# THE STEP NOT BEYOND

Suny Series, Intersections: Philosophy and Critical Theory
Rodolphe Gasché and Mark C. Taylor, editors

# THE STEP NOT BEYOND

Translation of *Le pas au-delà* by Maurice Blanchot.
Translated and with an introduction by
*Lycette Nelson*

State University of New York Press

Originally published in French as
*Le Pas Au-Delà* © Éditions Gallimard, 1973.

Published by
State University of New York Press, Albany

For information, address the State University of New York Press,
State University Plaza, Albany, NY 12246

**Library of Congress Cataloging-in-Publication Data**

Blanchot, Maurice.
   [Pas au-delà. English]
   The step not beyond / Maurice Blanchot : translated and with
an introduction by Lycette Nelson.
      p.   cm. — (Suny series. Intersections : philosophy and
critical theory)
   Translation of: Le pas au-delà.
   ISBN 0-7914-0907-4 (alk. paper). — ISBN 0-7914-0908-2
(pbk.
   :alk. paper)
   1. Blanchot. Maurice—Philosophy. 2. Literature—Philosophy.
I. Title. II. Series: Intersections (Albany, N.Y.)
PQ2603.L3343P313 1992
848'.91207—dc20                                                91-13269
                                                                   CIP

10   9   8   7   6   5   4   3   2   1

# INTRODUCTION

In 1971 Maurice Blanchot published a major collection of essays regrouped and, in some cases, revised, under the title *L'Entretien infini*. *L'Entretien infini* announces the project of "une parole plurielle," "plural speech" and puts the project into practise in its use of numerous strategies to introduce multiplicity into writing—the dialogue, the fragment, multiple typefaces—all forms of disruption, interruption and discontinuity. The fragmentary is the one of these forms that Blanchot develops the furthest in the two works that follow *L'Entretien infini: The Step Not Beyond,* published in French in 1973, and *The Writing of the Disaster,* published in 1980 (English translation by Ann Smock, University of Nebraska Press, 1986). To understand the place of *The Step Not Beyond* in Blanchot's work, we must see it as the culmination of a long development in Blanchot's thought centering around three major ideas: the fragment, the neuter, and the Eternal Return. This development can be traced through *L'Entretien infini,* particularly in such essays as "Sur un changement d'époque: l'exigence du retour," "Nietzsche et l'écriture fragmentaire" and "Parole de fragment." *The Writing of the Disaster* follows *The Step Not Beyond* in its use of the fragment and of different typefaces. Blanchot's use of the fragment is part of the overall project of *L'Entretien infini* to find a language that is truly multiple and that does not attempt to achieve closure.

Blanchot's first use of the fragmentary in a full-length work is in *L'Attente l'oubli* (1962), another pivotal text in his work as a whole. It is at once the first full-length fragmentary work and the last that can be characterized as fiction. What distinguishes Blanchot's use of the fragment in *L'Attente l'oubli* from his more developed use of it in *The Step Not Beyond* and *The Writing of the Disaster* is that its use in the later texts seems to arise out of a much more marked necessity in his own thought resulting from his readings of Nietzsche, and particularly of the idea of the Eternal Return.

The fragment is, in the first place, a challenge to unified, systematic thought. Françoise Collin notes in her preface to the second edition of *Maurice Blanchot et la question de l'écriture,*

> Since the first edition of this book [1971] there have been displacements of themes and of forms in the work of Maurice Blanchot, but not ruptures. Thus, reflection has taken the place of fiction, and has gone further and further away from commentary without moving away from dialogue. It has developed itself more and more in the form of the fragment— in the form of the archipelago—thus affirming all the more its resistance to totality and the system.[1]

Roger Laporte also remarks a change in Blanchot's writing beginning with *L'Attente l'oubli* and finding its achievement in *Le pas au-delà.* He writes,

> *L'Attente l'oubli,* a transitional work, marks the end of the novels and récits . . . Thus begins a third epoch marked by the publication of two major works: *Le pas au-delà* . . . and *L'écriture du désastre.* . . .In the same work alternate texts called "fictional" (but fictional in a sense that no longer has anything to do with the novelistic), texts printed in italics, and the texts in which literature—before I would have said "writing"—with its dramas, its stakes, its intrigue, its enigmas, bares itself . . . —task not vain, but impossible, as if in literature there were very little question of literature, but always of something else.[2]

As Laporte points out, both *The Step Not Beyond* and *The Writing of the Disaster,* while primarily theoretical fragmentary texts, have elements of fiction as well, disrupting the disruptiveness of the fragmentary even further in using multiple typefaces and multiple voices. We will see that in *The Step Not Beyond* there is a kind of *récit* that goes on within the italicized fragments. Thus, the mixing of genres that has always characterized Blanchot's work and made it impossible to categorize continues and is further radicalized in the later texts. It is in this sense that the fragmentary texts mark a shift, but not a rupture, in Blanchot's work, as remarked by both Collin and Laporte.

If there is agreement that a change takes place in Blanchot's writing, what brings about this change? From Blanchot's own notes to the essays on Nietzsche in *L'Entretien infini,* we know that he was very much influenced by several works on Nietzsche that appeared in France in the 1960s and '70s, as well as by the writings of Jacques Derrida. Blanchot writes in a footnote at the end of "Nietzsche et l'écriture fragmentaire": "These pages are written in the margins of several recent works of Michel Foucault, Gilles Deleuze, Eugen Fink, Jean Granier, and of several essays by Jacques Derrida collected under the title *Writing and Difference.*"[3] Another name that he mentions elsewhere as being very important in his understanding of the Eternal Return is that of Pierre Klossowski.

In the essay "Nietzsche et l'écriture fragmentaire," Blanchot explores the place of the fragment in Nietzsche's thought, as well as Nietzsche's relationship to Hegel and to traditional philosophy. Blanchot sees two contradictory tendencies in Nietzsche's thought: one toward, the other away from, systematization. While Gilles Deleuze, in *Nietzsche et la philosophie,* sees Nietzsche's relation to Hegel as oppositional, Blanchot emphasizes the necessity of the hegelian system for Nietzsche and views the ambiguity of Nietzsche's position regarding totality as the result of the impossibility of thinking apart from the system. Nietzsche's use of the fragment and the aphorism, even while attempting to oppose hegelian dialectics, represents for Blanchot a recognition that the hegelian whole has been completed. It is after the completion of the whole, in the "beyond" of philosophy, that fragmentary writing takes place.

The fragmentary does not precede the whole, but takes place *outside* the whole and after it. When Nietzsche affirms: *"Nothing exists outside the whole"* even if he means to lessen our guilty particularity and to reject judgement, measure, negation, it is still true that he thus affirms the question of the whole as the only tenable one and thus restores the idea of totality. Dialectics, the system, thought as thought of wholeness, are given back their rights, founding philosophy as completed discourse. But when he says, *"It seems important to me that one get rid of the whole, of unity, . . . we must smash the universe to pieces, lose our respect for the Whole"*, then he enters the space of the fragmentary and takes the risk of a thought that is no longer guaranteed by unity.[4]

What does it mean for fragmentary writing to come *after* the whole, that is, after the completion of time as history? Blanchot writes in *The Writing of the Disaster,* "If [fragmentary writing] claims that its time comes only after the whole—at least ideally—has been completed, this is because that time is never sure, but is the absence of time. . . ."[5] To understand the "after" of "after the whole", we must examine Blanchot's idea of the Eternal Return and the enormous consequences that result from it for him.

In the essay "Sur un changement d'époque: l'exigence du retour,"[6] Blanchot gives a brief catalogue of various commentators' responses to the Eternal Return, among them those of Heidegger, Georges Bataille and Pierre Klossowski. For Heidegger, the Eternal Return and the will to power are the two central ideas in Nietzsche's thought and are completely dependent on one another. This relation is summed up, if in a somewhat banalized form, in Nietzsche's famous "Will it if you can will to live it eternally", in which what seems to be at stake in the Eternal Return is the future as it is contained in the present moment.

For both Bataille and Klossowski, what is essential in the revelation of the Eternal Return is the revelation itself rather than what results form it. According to Blanchot, Bataille faulted Nietzsche for having tried to develop what was really a mystic experience into a scientific doctrine. Klossowski, on the other hand, poses the question of how a doctrine of the Eternal Return is even possible if the experience of it destroys the subject in whom it occurs and marks a rupture in thought and in time. This question has great implications for Blanchot, as he writes, "The question is developed in all its rigor, its breadth, and its authority by Pierre Klossowski. It is not only Nietzsche who receives new justice from this investigation, but through it, what is decided is a change so radical that we are incapable of mastering it, or even of suffering it."[7]

In Blanchot's understanding of the Eternal Return, the loss of identity of the subject occupies a central place. In *The Step Not Beyond* he develops at length the relation of the neuter, or neutral, to fragmentary writing and the Eternal Return. The essential feature of the neuter in Blanchot's overall critique of the idea of presence as all is its displacement of the subject in writing, which ultimately displaces the whole notion of the subject as the locus of self-presence. Beginning from the neuter, Blanchot displaces first the subject, then identity in general, and finally the present itself.

The neuter, or what Blanchot calls in *The Step Not Beyond* le *"il"*, the "he/it," taking the place of the subject in writing, detaches it from any relation to unity, displacing this relation in substituting for the I, always attached to a place, the he/it which is without place. The he/it can never be a speaking subject, can never have the presence of an I. The neuter displaces the subject as a rule of identity by introducing rupture into the idea of the self as presence and self-presence. If the he/it can substitute for any I, then the I is not full, living presence, but only "a canonic abbreviation for a rule of identity." Blanchot asks: if he/it replaces the I, does it not become only another I, still determined by identity? Or does it, on the other hand, put itself in dialectical opposition to the One, "therefore including itself conveniently in the whole"? The neuter maintains the law of identity unless, Blanchot answers,

> . . . he/it, specified as the indeterminate term in order that the self in turn might determine itself as the major determinant, the never–subjected subject, is the very *relation* of the self to the other, in this sense: infinite or discontinuous, in this sense: relation always in displacement and in displacement in regard to itself, displacement also of that which would be without place. (SNB,5)

In this relation the I is forced to accept itself, "not only as hypothetical, even fictional, but as a canonic abbreviation, representing the law of the same, fractured in advance . . ." (SNB,6)

The Eternal Return of the Same says that the same will return to the same. If the same is always displaced in relation to itself, however, there is no place to which it could return. The same, in the form of the self, occurs as present to itself, but, in Blanchot's formulation of the return, there is no present in which the self could be present. It is in this sense that Blanchot's thought of the return is radical in its departure from that of other commentators. What is terrifying about the Eternal Return is not that what I live now I will live eternally, but that there is not, and never has been, any now in which to live anything.

To think the Eternal Return, one must think time as an infinite recurrence of finitude, but if the return is eternal, the circulation it brings about is never circulation of the same—of a full present—but only repetition without origin. The law of the return tells us that in the future will recur what has occurred, not in the present, but in the past, since everything that can happen has already happened. The infinity supposed by the return is not the eternity of the full present, but the infinity of rupture that the lack of the present introduces into time. Blanchot writes,

> The law of the return supposing that "everything" would come again, seems to take time as completed: the circle out of circulation of all circles; but, in as much as it breaks the ring in its middle, it proposes a time not uncompleted, a time, on the contrary, finite, except in the present point that alone we think we hold, and that, lacking, introduces rupture into infinity, making us live as in a state of perpetual death. (SNB,12)

The impossibility of thinking the Eternal Return arises from the necessity of thinking time as both finite and infinite in order to think it. One must think time as completed in order to think the Eternal Return. However, if time can only realize itself in the fullness of presence, time can never be completed if the present is lacking. The circulation of the return becomes a circulation of a rupture always contained in the time of the circulation—an absent moment that creates a supplement of time. The completed time of Hegel gets recirculated in Nietzsche's Eternal Return, but in that very circulation it can never be thought of as fully realized. When Blanchot says that Nietzsche can only come after Hegel, but that "it is always before and always after Hegel that he comes and that he comes again," he expresses the complete paradox of the Eternal Return.

> Nietzsche, (if his name serves to name the law of the Eternal Return) and Hegel (if his name invites us to think presence as all and the all as presence) allow us to sketch a mythology: Nietzsche can only come after Hegel, but it is always before and always after Hegel that he comes and comes again. Before: since, even though it is thought as absolute, presence has never gathered in itself the realized totality of knowledge; presence knows itself . . . only as a present unsatisfied practically, unreconciled with presence as all; thus is not Hegel only a pseudo–Hegel? And Nietzsche always comes after because the law he brings supposes the completion of time as present and in this completion its absolute destruction, such that the Eternal Return . . . freeing the future of any present and the past of any presence, shatters thought up to this infinite affirmation: in the future will return infinitely what in no form and never could be present, in the same way that, in the past, that which in the past never belonged in any form to the present has returned (SNB,22)

What is left of time when the present is taken out of it? We would seem to be left with one time that repeats itself over and over—not two modalities of time that repeat and anticipate one another, but only one. Yet we cannot think past and future as identical without presence. The future, in repeating the past, is never identical to it, says Blanchot, "even if they are the same." Past and future are not interchangeable, but disjunct.

The Eternal Return marks time as ruptured and leaves the point of rupture unbridged and unbridgeable. It introduces a time that disrupts all of thought's tendencies to unity and totalization. Fragmentary writing, as discontinuous and disruptive, corresponds to this time and responds to the demand of the return. The relation of fragmentary writing to the whole becomes clearer in the context of the Eternal Return. Fragmentary writing occurs when knowledge becomes uncertain of itself, when the past cannot become present to consciousness. While it should know everything, because everything that can happen has already happened, it can know nothing actually. As Walter Benjamin observes in comparing mechanized labor to gambling, in any repetitive act, knowledge and experience are useless, since one can learn nothing from one throw of the dice or one turn of the machine to the next. When the future repeats the past without the intermediary of the present, the past becomes useless for knowledge. Knowledge takes on the structure of the phrase repeated several times in *The Step Not Beyond:* "I don't know, but I have the feeling that I am going to have known," spoken both in the future and in the past, as both a prophecy and a memory (I remembered this phrase: "I don't know, but have the feeling that I am going to have known."), but never as present knowledge.

The rupture of the present created by the Eternal Return frees writing from any dependence on speech as presence by destroying the foundation that presence would supposedly provide for it. Without this foundation, it no longer plays the role of follower to speech. Writing responds to the demand of the return because, as Blanchot has insisted throughout his theoretical work, writing never begins, but is always beginning again. The time of the Eternal Return is the time of writing, which will be read in the future and will have been written in the past.

> The demand of the return would then be the demand of a time without present, time that would also be that of writing, future time, past time, which the radical disjunction of one from the other, even if they are the same, keeps from identifying other than as the difference repetition brings. (SNB,16)

Blanchot moves, through his thinking of the Eternal Return, towards an idea of writing as difference. The Eternal Return is repetition, not of the same, but of difference, a point which Gilles Deleuze makes quite explicitly: ". . . identity in the eternal return does not designate the nature of what comes again, but, on the contrary, the fact of coming again for that which differs."[8] Blanchot has, since his earliest writings, repeated the idea that writing is repetition without origin. Through the Eternal Return he arrives at the idea of repetition as the repetition of difference, and of writing as difference. Blanchot writes in "Nietzsche et l'écriture fragmentaire":

> One can suppose that if thought in Nietzsche needed force conceived as *"play of forces and waves of forces"* to think plurality and to think difference . . . this is because it supports the suspicion that difference is movement, or, more exactly, that it determines the time and the becoming in which it inscribes itself, as the Eternal Return would make us think that difference is experienced as repetition and that repetition is difference. Difference is not an intemporal rule, the fixity of law. It is . . . space in as much as it *"spaces itself and disseminates itself"* and time: not the directed homogeneity of becoming, but becoming when *"it scands itself, signifies itself"*, interrupts itself, and, in this interruption, does not continue, but dis–continues itself; from which we must conclude that difference, play of time and space, is the silent play of relations . . . that regulates writing, which is to affirm bravely that difference, essentially, writes.[9]

Blanchot's references to the writings of Jacques Derrida are evident here. Blanchot uses certain Derridean ideas to make his own thought more precise, as we will see in his use of the notion of the trace in *The Step Not Beyond*. While he uses many of the same terms as Derrida, there are marked divergences in his use of them.

Without going through the whole history of the notion of the trace as it is used first by Emmanuel Levinas and then by Derrida,[10] let us look briefly at what Levinas and Derrida define the trace to be. Levinas defines the trace in "The Trace of the Other" as the trace of ". . . that which properly speaking has never been there, of what is always past."[11] The trace in Levinas is related quite specifically to a transcendant being, to an other who is absolutely other. It is Levinas' trace which, "reconciled to a Heideggerian intention" signifies for Derrida ". . . the undermining of an ontology which, in its innermost course, has determined the meaning of being as presence and the meaning of language as speech."[12]

In the essay "Différance," Derrida articulates the relationship of the trace to the arche–trace and of the arche–trace to the impossibility of an originary presence. What is constitutive of the trace for Derrida, as for Levinas, is its erasure. While Derrida poses the problem of how anything could ever have been present in an originary way through the trace and the arche–trace, Blanchot approaches the impossibility of an originary presence through the Eternal Return and places the trace within the time of the return. Blanchot introduces the trace thus:

> Effaced before being written. If the word trace can be admitted, it is as the index that would indicate as erased what was, however, never traced. All our writing . . . would be this: the anxious search for what was never written in the present, but in a past to come. (SNB,17)

The trace signifies for Blanchot, as for Derrida, the lack of an origin, because the trace never refers back to an original marking. Blanchot distinguishes the trace from the mark.

> . . . writing marks, but does not leave marks. More precisely, there is between mark and traces such a difference that it almost accounts for the equivocal nature of writing. Writing marks and leaves traces, but the traces do not depend on the mark, and, at the limit, are not in relation to it. (SNB,53)

While Roger Laporte hazards the suggestion that the mark in Blanchot, the trace in Levinas, and the arche–trace in Derrida all refer to the same thing,[13] it is hard to read this in Blanchot's use of the terms "mark" and "trace". When he says, for instance,

> The mark, it is to be missing from the present and to make the present lack. And the trace, being always traces, does

not refer to any initial presence that would still be there as remainder or vestige, there where it has disappeared. (SNB,54)

there is nothing of Derrida's idea of the trace as constitutive of the present. What Blanchot really insists on in his use of the trace is the idea of writing as effacement, as opposed to the traditional idea that writing preserves what would otherwise disappear. He begins his discussion of the trace with the haunting claim, "Everything will efface itself, everything must efface itself."[14] In fact, it seems that one of the aims of the fragmentary is to make writing efface itself all the more definitively. The lack of continuity between the past and the future means a forgetting that writing, rather than preserving anything against it, only exacerbates.

> Writing is not destined to leave traces, but to erase, by traces, all traces, to disappear in the fragmentary space of writing more definitely than one disappears in the tomb . . . (SNB,50)

One of the uses of the idea of the trace to which Derrida refers, in addition to Levinas' and Nietzsche's, is Freud's. For Freud, the trace is the mark of difference as it can be seen by the existence of memory. For Blanchot, the trace seems to have more to do with forgetting than with remembering, ". . . as if between past and future, the absence of present ruled in the simplified form of forgetfulness." (SNB,16)

The trace takes on a particular significance in *The Step Not Beyond* when seen in its relation to the *pas* of the title *Le pas au-delà,* which refers to a whole series of ideas common in Blanchot's thought: the thought of the limit, prohibition and transgression, the negation of negation, which Derrida analyzes in his essay "Pas". The trace is at once tracing and effacement, the *pas* at once prohibition and transgression. Blanchot writes in *The Writing of the Disaster,* "Passivity, passion, past, *pas* (at once negation and the trace or movement of an advance), this semantic play gives us the slippage of meaning, but nothing that we could trust as an answer that would satisfy us."[15] In "Pas," Derrida looks at the dissemination and interrelation of two words in Blanchot's work: *viens* and *pas*. He focuses on the dissemination of the *pas* in the title *Le pas au-delà*, the work going by that name, and Blanchot's work as a whole (the word or the sound "pas" appears in several of Blanchot's titles: *Faux pas, Celui qui ne m'accompagnait pas, L'Espace littéraire, La part du feu*).

Derrida asks, speaking of the title, "How would you translate this displacement, this play of words and of things, I mean, into another language?"[16] The *pas* presents problems in translation not only because its meaning is double and its use in the phrase *le pas au-delà* ambiguous, but also because, as Derrida points out, the play is not just a play of words, but of words and things. The possibilities for translating the whole title are actually quadruple, since both *pas* and *au-delà* can be taken either as nouns or adverbs (*pas* is both a step and part of the negative adverb *ne-pas; au-delà* means "beyond," but also occurs as "l'au-delà," the beyond); the meaning of the entire phrase changes depending on the semantic function of each of its parts. However one chooses to translate *pas,* it is impossible to preserve the two meanings *at once,* although the simultaneity of meanings in the same word is important in preserving the sense of prohibition and transgression occurring at the same time. As the trace is effaced as it is written, so the *pas* both creates and erases the limit in its crossing. This is perhaps even more clear in the use of the phrase *faux pas* (false step) and its homonym *faut pas* (do not, you must not). Because of the double meaning of *pas,* every step becomes a false step.

The phrase *le pas au-delà* appears within the text both as *le pas au-delà* and as *le "pas au-delà,"* the first seeming to refer to the step, and the second to its injunction. However, as Derrida points out, one can never tell exactly what the quotation marks in the phrase *le "pas au-delà"* refer to, nor when this phrase is being cited even where there are no quotation marks. The relation between signifier and signified is very ambiguous—is what is signified in *le "pas au-delà"* a phrase or a thing?—made doubly ambiguous both by the quotation marks and by the definite article, which makes the prohibition *pas au-delà* (not beyond, do not go beyond) into a substantive.

Derrida warns against taking the *pas* only in it function of negating, even if this is understood to be non-dialectical. Among several reasons he gives for not doing so, the most important is that:

> ... in isolating ... the logical or semantic function of the *ne-pas*, in separating it ... both from the semantic of the "pas" of walking and from the non-semantic (contaminations, anomalies, delirium, etc.) one forbids oneself all that leads the problematic of logic, of dialectic, of meaning, the being of the entity (philosophy and its *pas au-delà*, thought) towards a coming of the event (as distancing of the near) [Ereignis, Entferrung, Enteignis] "before" which philosophy and its *pas au-delà*, thought, forces itself, without ever succeeding, to close itself.[17]

Philosophy demands a beyond, a point of totalization, of completion and closure. The *pas* does not simply negate such a possibility, but puts into question the possibility of negation necessary for closure to be accomplished. How can this *pas* ever produce closure if it sets up a limit to be crossed even in prohibiting its crossing?

The step beyond is never completed, or, if it is completed, is never beyond. Transgression never really transgresses, but only calls for another limit.

> The circle of the law is this: there must be a crossing in order for there to be a limit, but only the limit, in as much as uncrossable, summons to cross, affirms the desire (the false step) that has always already, through an unforeseeable movement, crossed the line. (SNB,24)

Transgression cannot be accomplished because there is no present in which the prohibition against crossing the limit could be pronounced or in which the crossing itself could take place. Blanchot in fact suggests that the present is nothing but this line to be crossed. The strange structure of the *pas*, of prohibition and transgression, must be placed within the time of the Eternal Return. The law presupposes a trinary time in which the prohibition is first pronounced, then recognized, then broken. As the time of the return lacks this temporal structure, the prohibition does not precede the transgression, but occurs simultaneously with it and works in such a way as to efface the limits imposed by a time structured by the present.

The transgression that is never accomplished is, primarily, dying. Blanchot looks at the kinds of prohibition that exist against dying and the kind of transgression that dying represents. Dying is a transgression against and out of time, because there is no time for dying. Dying can never be completed because it lacks the solidity of an event. It does not occur through any decisiveness or action, but only through the most passive passivity. Dying, like writing, cannot take place in the present because the limit that dying represents cannot be situated. Not only is dying in the present forbidden, but the present, as prohibited, is what prevents dying from taking place.

> . . . one could affirm: it is forbidden to die *in the present.*"— "Which means also: the present does not die and there is no present for dying. It is the present that would in some way pronounce the prohibition." . . . —"Thus a time without present would be 'affirmed' according to the demand of the return."—"This is why even transgression does not accomplish itself." (SNB,107–108)

The prohibition can never be broken by a transgressive act, which would only affirm the prohibitiveness of the prohibition. Instead it is only through the most passive passivity that the prohibition would lose its prohibitive force. Dying is the step/not beyond that is never accomplished, that one seeks to accomplish in the other, dying in the other's death. The *pas au-delà* transforms the *pas* of negation into the *pas* of patience, passion, and passivity, taking its power of negation away through the powerlessness of the unaccomplished. The *pas* of the completely passive is transgressive without accomplishing anything. Pure passivity is what is least allowed. We seek passivity in the other, by dying in the place of the other.

Dying in the other sets us free from ourselves, but does not change our relation to dying, which is anonymous, intransitive, disappropriating, and therefore without relation to any I, be it mine or the other's.

Passivity, patience, passion open the relation to the other in refusing the *pas* of the negative.

> Patience opens me entirely, all the way to a passivity that is the *pas* of the utterly passive, and that has therefore abandoned the level of life where *passive* would simply be the opposite of active.[18]

Dying in the other is never accomplished, yet the attempt to reach the other in his death makes me in some way responsible for that death. Blanchot returns to this theme in a later work, *La communauté inavouable,* where he writes,

> To maintain myself present in proximity to the other who distances himself definitively in dying, to take upon myself the death of the other as the only death that concerns me, this is what places me outside myself and is the only separation that can open me, in its impossibility, to the Open of a community.[19]

The relation to the other is the main focus of the italicized fragments of *The Step Not Beyond,* in which two unnamed figures speak to one another about some anonymous and very indefinite others whose approach they await. Their wait for these others is a figure for the approach of their own deaths, or death, since they attempt to die in one another's place. When "they"—these others—finally arrive, there is no time for this event, as there is no time for dying, although death has all time at its disposal. The attempt to reach the other, to die in his death, is the attempt to "go beyond." If we cannot accomplish this it is because we are never passive enough. The passivity of dying is itself a "beyond," beyond negativity and always beyond us. The limit it poses is effaced in dying itself.

When one of the figures of the italicized fragments finally dies, it is as if nothing had happened. *"He was so calm in dying that he seemed, before dying, already dead, after and forever, still alive . . . thus having effaced the limit at the mo-*

*ment in which it is it that effaces."* (SNB,137) This event, however uneventful, nevertheless provides the basis for an appeal to the ethical. Whether one can take responsibility for another's death, what it means to live or die for others, whether death is light or heavy—all of these are questions that are given meaning only by the erasure of death as a limit. All of the meaning that we give to such questions is given by the anticipation of the event of dying, and not by the event (or non-event) itself. It is only when dying is understood as the limit that is effaced "at the moment in which it is it that effaces," that there can be an appeal to an ethics that is not weighty, that does not give death a gravity it does not have, that does not pose death as the ultimate prohibition.

## NOTES

1. Françoise Collin, *Maurice Blanchot et la question de l'écriture,* Preface to the second edition, Gallimard, 1986, p. 7

2. Roger Laporte, *Maurice Blanchot: L'Ancien, l'effroyablement ancien,* Fata Morgana, 1987, note 15, p. 66

3. Maurice Blanchot, *L'Entretien infini,* Gallimard, 1969, note, p. 255

4. Op. cit., p. 229

5. Maurice Blanchot, *The Writing of the Disaster,* translated by Ann Smock, University of Nebraska, 1986, pp. 59–60

6. Blanchot, *L'Entretien infini,* pp. 394–418

7. Op. cit., p. 408

8. Gilles Deleuze, *Nietzsche et la philosophie,* P.U.F., 1962, pp. 54–55

9. Blanchot, *L'Entretien infini,* p. 242

10. For a discussion of the trace in Derrida and Levinas, and of Derrida's relation to Levinas, see Robert Bernasconi, "The Trace of Levinas in Derrida" in *Derrida and Différance,* edited by David Wood and Robert Bernasconi, Northwestern University, 1988. For a detailed discussion of Derrida's use of the trace and the archetrace see also Rodolphe Gasché, *The Tain of the Mirror,* Harvard University Press, pp. 186–194

11. Emmanuel Levinas, "The Trace of the Other", in *Deconstruction and Criticism,* edited by Mark Taylor, University of Chicago, 1986, p. 358

12. Jacques Derrida, *Of Grammatology,* translated by Gayatari Spivak, Johns Hopkins, 1976, p. 7

13. Laporte, *Maurice Blanchot: L'Ancien, l'effroyablement ancien,* note 19, p. 73

14. This is the subject of a recent essay by Roger Laporte in the special issue of *Lignes* on Blanchot. See Laporte, "Tout doit s'effacer, tout s'effacera" in *Lignes,* no. 11, September 1990

15. Blanchot, *The Writing of the Disaster,* p. 16

16. Derrida, *Parages,* Galilée, 1986, p. 53

17. Ibid.

18. Blanchot, *The Writing of the Disaster,* p. 13

19. Blanchot, *La communauté inavouable,* Editions de Minuit, 1983, p. 21

Let us enter into this relation.

♦     To death we are not accustomed.

♦     Death being that to which we are not accustomed, we approach it either as the unaccustomed that astonishes or as the unfamiliar that horrifies. The thought of death does not help us to think death, does not give us death as something to think. Death, thought, close to one another to the extent that thinking, we die, if, dying, we excuse ourselves from thinking: every thought would be mortal; each thought, the last thought.

♦     Time, time: the step not beyond that is not accomplished in time would lead outside of time, without this outside being intemporal, but there where time would fall, fragile fall, according to this "outside of time in time" towards which writing would attract us, were we allowed, having disappeared from ourselves, to write within the secret of the ancient fear.

♦     From where does it come, this power of uprooting, of destruction or change, in the first words written facing the sky, in the solitude of the sky, words by themselves without prospect or pretense: "it—the sea"?
    It is certainly satisfying (too satisfying) to think that, by the mere fact that something like these words, "it—the sea" is written, with the demand that results from them and from which they also result, that somewhere the possibility of a

radical transformation is inscribed, be it for a single one—the possibility, that is, of its suppression as a personal existence. Possibility: nothing more.

Do not draw any consequences from these words written one day (which were, or could have been, at once and just as well, some other words), nor even from the demand to write, to suppose that this had been entrusted to you, as you persuade yourself and sometimes dissuade yourself that it had: all that you could hold onto of it would only serve to unify, in a presumptuous way, an existence insignificant, and (by the proposition of this demand of writing itself) nevertheless removed somewhat from unity. Do not hope, if there lies your hope—and one must suspect it—to unify your existence, to introduce into it, in the past, some coherence, by way of the writing that disunifies.

◆    To write as a question of writing, question that bears the writing that bears the question, no longer allows you this relation to the being—understood in the first place as tradition, order, certainty, truth, any form of taking root—that you received one day from the past of the world, domain you had been called upon to govern in order to strengthen your "Self", although this was as if fissured, since the day when the sky opened upon its void.

I will try in vain to represent him to myself, he who I was not and who, without wanting to, began to write, writing (and knowing it then) in such a way that the pure product of doing nothing was introduced into the world and into his world. That happened "at night". During the day there were the daytime acts, the day to day words, the day to day writing, affirmations, values, habits, nothing that counted and yet something that one had confusedly to call life. The certainty that in writing he was putting between parentheses precisely this certainty, including the certainty of himself as the subject of writing, led him slowly, though right away, into an empty space whose void (the barred zero, heraldic) in no way prevented the turns and detours of a very long process.

2

♦     *In this city, he knew there were people who did not see anyone, and so he had to ask himself: how did he know it? Perhaps it was not something that he knew, but that was included in knowledge. Knowing anything else meant having to know it in advance or not know it. How, given this, resist the temptation—the desire—to go look for them? "How does one go about meeting them?"—"Well, nothing could be more simple: you will stumble upon them."*

*They were several, of that, also, he could be sure; several, living together, or together and separate? Several—perhaps this only helped him not to think of them in an overly determined way: some people.*

*"You mean, by chance?"—But he repeated: "You will stumble upon them." Naturally, before even speaking of it to him and especially since speaking of it to him, he had anticipated another answer: "You know them." By which he would have understood that to know them was not the best way to meet them. But when he had decided, as though under the pressure of common words, to ask, "Do you think I know them?", he was surprised by the frivolity of the answer. "How could that be, you don't see anybody?"*

*At least he saw him, even if, when he thought about it, he could foresee how, saying this to him—but he would not say it—he would have been answered: "Just as I was saying, you don't see anybody."*


♦     Weak thoughts, weak desires: he felt their force.


♦     The relation to the "he/it"[1]: the plurality that the "he/it" holds is such that it cannot be marked by any plural sign; why? "they" [*ils*] would still designate an analyzable, and thus maniable, whole. "They" is the way in which ("he/it") frees him-/it-self from the neuter by borrowing from the plurality the possibility of determining itself, thus returning conveniently to indeterminacy, as if (he/it) could find the mark adequate to fix it a place—that very determined one in which every undetermined inscribes itself.

If I write he/it, denouncing it rather than indicating it, far from giving it a rank, a role or presence which would elevate it above anything that could designate it, it is I who, from this, enter into the relation in which "I" accepts solidification into a fictional or functional identity, in order that the game of writing may be played, of which he/it is either the partner and (at the same time) the product or the gift, or the bet, the stake, which, as such, principle player, plays, changes, displaces itself and takes the place of the change itself, displacement that lacks placing and that is missing from any placing.

◆   he/it: if I remain at the border of writing, careful not to introduce him/it in capitalized form, more careful still not to make it carry an excess of meaning that would come to it from one's not knowing what it designates, this word that I maintain, not without struggle, in the position I momentarily assign to it (at the border of writing), I not only have to watch over it constantly, but, starting from it, by an impossible usurpation or fiction, to watch over the change of place and the configuration that would result from it for this "self", from the start charged with representing the same and the identity or permanence of signs in and by their graphism, while at the same time having no other form than this function or puncturing of identity. The self is not a self but the same of myself[2], not some personal, impersonal identity, sure and vacillating, but the law or rule that conventionally assures the ideal identity of terms or notations. The self is therefore an abbreviation that one could call canonical, a formula that regulates and, if you like, blesses, in the first person, the pretention of the Same to primacy. Whence, perhaps, the sacred character that is attached to the self and that egoism confiscates, giving it the privilege of the central place it would occupy, and making it the fundamental trait of any movement to bring together, to associate, to group, to unify, or even, negatively, to disunify, to dissociate, to disassemble.

But does he/it, other than by subtraction, let itself escape the limitless sphere where the attraction of the canonic abbreviation of the self would exert itself, there where, under what-

4

ever form, identity rules? If he/it becomes the other, does it not become only another self characterized by the indirect (though in no way secondary) complex relation from which it comes and which it supports, or does it only become, at best, at worst, that from which the One would be absent, and which readily marks itself as not-One (the negation ordering itself in its turn by a rigorous sign of exclusion and thereby including itself conveniently in the whole)? Unless he/it, specified as the indeterminate term in order that the self in turn might determine itself as the major determinant, the never-subjected subject, is the very *relation* of the self to the other, in this sense: infinite or discontinuous, in this sense: relation always in displacement, and in displacement in regard to itself, without anything that has to displace itself, displacement also of that which would be without place. A word perhaps, nothing but a word, but a word in excess, a word too many, which for that reason is always lacking. Nothing but a word.


♦     Why does it exert this non-attraction on him? he/it: let us admit that it is not content to take the place left empty by the major determinant (the non-subjected subject). Is it content to leave the place empty, marking it with an all too visible blank, like a slot that is easy to fill? But it no more leaves it blank by filling it with a seeming word, substitute of a substitute, a pronoun that, indicating nothing but the void, would signify it as all the more void in that the void would not appear, being occupied by the non-term that is nevertheless not simply undetermined.

Does "he/it" indicate "it"-self better in the double use that this sentence has just made of it, either as a repetition, which is not one (the second "it", if it restores the first, gives it back to set the verb again in an unstable position—will it fall to one side or to the other?—which is the interrogative position), that is, an enunciation one might call "pleonastic", not because it would be pure redundancy, but because it is as if useless there, effacing itself, and effacing itself again, until it becomes lost in the inarticulation of the sentence?

♦    he/it: at the border of writing; transparency, as such, opaque; bearing what inscribes it, effacing it, effacing itself in the inscription, effacement of the mark that marks it; neuter under the spell of the neuter to the point of seeming dangerously to fix it and, if we were capable of "following" it up to this border where what writes itself has always already disappeared (see-sawed, capsized) in the neutrality of writing, to seem to tempt us to have a relation to that which excludes itself from any relation and which nevertheless indicates itself as absolute only in the relative mode (of the relation itself, multiple).

Whether capitalized or small, in the position of the subject, in the state of a pleonasm, indicating some other or no other, or indicating nothing but its own indication, the he/it without identity; personal? impersonal? not yet and always beyond; and not being someone or something, no more than it could have the magic of being or the fascination of non-being as a guarantee. For the moment, the only thing to say: he/it, a word too many, which by a ruse we place at the border of writing, or the relation of writing to writing, when writing indicates itself at its own border.

♦    Non-present, non-absent; it tempts us in the manner of that which we would not know how to meet, save in situations which we are no longer in: save—save at the limit, situations we call "extreme", assuming there are any.

♦    The relation of the self to the other, difficult to think (relation that the he/it would "relate") because of the status of the other, sometimes and at once the other as term, sometimes and at once the other as relation without term, relay always to be relayed; then, by the change that it proposes to "me", "me" having thus to accept itself not only as hypothetical, even fictional, but as a canonic abbreviation, representing the law of the same, fractured in advance (thus again—according to the fallacious proposition of this morcellated self, injured intimately—again a living, that is to say, full, self).

6

◆     *As if there would have reverberated, in a muffled way, a* call.

◆     At the border of writing, always having to live without you.

◆     *It was almost easy for him, there where he lived, to live almost without a sign, almost without a self, as if at the border of writing; close to this word, barely a word, rather a word too many, and in that nothing but a word from which, one day in the past, gently welcomed, he had received the salute that did not save, the summons that had awakened him. That could be told, even if, and especially if, nobody were there to hear it. In a certain way, he would have liked to be able to treat it with the gentleness he had received from it, a gentleness that held him at a distance, because of the excessive power it gave him over himself, and, by way of him, over all things. Over almost all things: there was always this slight restriction, implied, which obliged him—sweet obligation—to go back, often and as if by a ritual at which he smiled, to these ways of speaking, almost, maybe, barely, momentarily, unless, and many others, signs without signification that he knew very well (did he know it?) granted him something precious, the possibility of repeating himself—but no, he did not know what would come to him through them, "maybe" the right to cross the limit without his knowing it, "maybe" the anxious, slovenly retreat in face of the decisive affirmation from which they preserved him in order that he still be there not to hear it.*

◆     *As if there had reverberated, in a muffled way, this call, a call nevertheless joyful, the cry of children playing in the garden: "who is me today?" "who holds the place of me?" and the answer, joyful, infinite:* him, him, him.

◆     *The thought that had led him to the edge of awakening: nothing was forbidden to him, ruses, frauds, habits, lies,*

7

*truths, save (another one of those words on which he was used to relying), save—. And he was not fooled, even this law could turn around, leaving it intact, safe, it also.*

♦     *"We would give them a name."—"They would have one."—"The name we would give them would not be their real name."—"All the same, able to name them."—"Able to make it known that, the day they would recognize that they were ready, there would be a name for their name."—"A name such that there would be no place for them to feel summoned by it, nor tempted to respond to it, nor even ever denominated by this name."—"However, have we not assumed that they would have one name that would be common to them?"—"We have, but only so that they might more easily pass unnoticed."—"Then how could we know we could address ourselves to them? They are far away, you know."—"It is for this that we have names, more numerous and more marvellous than all those that one commonly uses."—"They wouldn't know it was their name."— "How could they know it; they don't have one."*

♦     *It was like an eternal subject of pleasantry, an innocent game: "You met them in the street?"—"Not exactly in the street: near the river, looking at books, then leaving or losing themselves in the crowd."—"That could not but be so; and, rather young, aren't they?"—"Young?" One had to stop at this word which involved, demanded, and promised too much; he did not concede it willingly until he let himself go ahead and answer: "Yes, young, there was no other word; and yet, young without anything that makes their age a moment of themselves, or youth a characteristic of age; young, but as in another time, thus not so young, as if youth made them ancient or too new to be able to appear only young."—"How you have observed them; did you have time? was it possible? is it possible?"—"It was not, in fact, but neither was it possible to meet them."*
*It was true that, when he leaves him, following street after street, streets bright, animated, not servile, he sees nobody, but*

8

*this is only a consequence of what he calls his immortality, and that he could more generously call the kindness of all, who let him pass, giving him their faces—how these faces are beautiful, would be beautiful if he saw them—a light, the burst of a happiness, of a distress.*

♦  *An imperfect remembrance? an absolute lie? a staggering truth? a silent desire?*

♦  *. . . sick or simply meditative; forgetting by a gift of forgetting that made each of his words, pronounced in a distinct manner, a surprise, a final truth, perhaps a painful wait; still, robust, unshakable.*

♦  He desired to say it to him: *this way of thinking about what he wanted to say even in saying it—to whom? or in saying that he would say it—to whom? even though he had gotten this way of thinking or thought he had gotten it from this point where it seemed he could fictitiously situate it, helped to hold him back from saying it. For he had to be there—in this place where it was given him to stay, like an assigned residence, in order for the other to be over there, immobile, immovable, yet always hard to recognize, as if the right to identity had been refused him at the same time it was granted to him.*
He desired to say it to him: *but how desire to speak, without the desire, and always in advance, destroying speech, even the most calm desire for the most calm speech? And still, he desired to say it, he would say it.*

♦  By what right, by what usurped power, had he planned this meeting, and, planning it, made it inevitable, or, on the contrary, impossible? "It was only a thought."—"Of course."—"But also a desire, something that one could not think but in

9

desiring it."—"Without being able to desire it, without being sure that one desired it."—"At the risk of speaking about it, with the suspicion that to speak about it was always to speak prematurely by an unfortunate indiscretion."—"Fortunate also; it was necessary."—"Was it necessary?"—"We'll know later."—"We'll know too late."

Speak, desire, meet: he realized that, playing with these three words (and, in this way, introducing the missing fourth, the game of the missing one), he could not produce one before, or rather than, the other two, except if playing it first did not in any way give it a primary role, not even that of a card sacrificed with a view to a strategy. A game that would perhaps consist of holding them together, without being able to hold them as elements of equal value, nor of unequal value, nor as the related particulars of the *same* game—which destroyed the game from the start, unless this game, becoming a game of destruction, in this way immediately acquired an immediately faulty preeminence. This remains true nevertheless: he must have met them (in one way or another, it hardly matters) in order to be able to speak about them; he must have met them to desire to meet them (or to feel that he could have desired it), and it was necessary, in order for him to meet them (even if he never meets them) that desire prepare him and speech dispose him to it, by the space that each of these occupies, and without the void from which the meeting would fill itself, would accomplish itself, in the way of an historic event.

◆     *In the cold happiness of his memory, as if memory were of everyone, forgetting of no one.*

◆     *Had he then forgotten it, the meeting always to come that had, however, always already taken place, in an eternal past, eternally without present? How could he have come to an instant of presence, if time's—their time's—detour was to deprive them of any relation to a present? Strict law, the highest of laws, such that, itself being submitted to it, it could not find the moment in which to apply itself, and, applying itself, to affirm itself. With one exception? Was not this exception, precisely and insidiously offered, temptation destined to tempt the law, like the thought that he would come, even with these three words, to the end of this same thought?*

♦    Know only—injunction that does not present itself—that the law of the return, counting for all of the past and all of the future, will never allow you, except through a misunderstanding, to leave yourself a place in a possible present, nor to let any presence come as far as you.

♦    *"I am afraid": that was what he happened to hear him say, barely having crossed the threshold, and what was frightening was the calm speech that seemed to use the "I" only to be afraid.*

♦    The Eternal Return of the Same: the same, that is to say, myself, in as much as it sums up the rule of identity, that is, the present self. But the demand of the return, excluding any present mode from time, would never release a now in which the same would come back to the same, to myself.

♦    The Eternal Return of the Same: as if the return, ironically proposed as the law of the Same, where the Same would be sovereign, did not necessarily make time an infinite game with two openings (given as one, and yet never unified): future always already past, past always still to come, from which the third instance, the instant of presence, excluding itself, would exclude any possibility of identity.

How, according to the law of the return, there where between past and future nothing is conjoined, leap from one to the other, when the rule does not allow any passage from one to the other, even that of a leap? The past, one says, would be the same as the future. There would be, then, only one modality, or a double modality functioning in such a way that identity, differed/deferred, would regulate the difference. But such would be the demand of the return: it is *"under a false appearance of a present"* that the ambiguity past-future would invisibly separate the future from the past.

♦     *They knew—according to the law of the return—that only the name, the event, the figure of death, would give, at the moment of disappearing in it, a right to presence: this is why they said they were immortal.*

♦     Let there be a past, let there be a future, with nothing that would allow the passage from one to the other, such that the line of demarcation would unmark them the more, the more it remained invisible: hope of a past, completed of a future. All that would remain of time, then, would be this line to cross, always already crossed, although not crossable, and, in relation to "me", unsuitable. Perhaps what we would call the "present" is only the impossibility of situating this line.

The law of the return supposing that "everything" would come again, seems to take time as completed: the circle out of circulation of all circles; but, in as much as it breaks the ring in its middle, it proposes a time not uncompleted, but, on the contrary, finite, except in the present point that alone we think we hold, and that, lacking, introduces rupture into infinity, making us live as in a state of perpetual death.

♦     *For having always lacked the present, the event had always disappeared without leaving any trace but that of a hope for the past, to the point of making the future the prophecy of an empty past.*

◆    The past (empty), the future (empty), in the false light of the present: only episodes to inscribe in and by the absence of any book.


◆    *The room was dark, not that it was obscure: the light was almost too visible, it did not illuminate.*


◆    *The calm word, carrying fear.*


◆    *He knew it (in accordance, perhaps, with the law):* the past is empty, and only the multiple play of mirroring, the illusion that there would be a present destined to pass and to hold itself back in the past, would lead one to believe that the past was filled with events, a belief that would make it appear less unfriendly, less frightening: a past thus inhabited, even if by phantoms, would grant the right to live innocently (in the narrative mode, which, once, twice, as many times as one time can repeat itself, makes its evocation usable) the very thing which, nevertheless, gives itself as revoked forever and, at the same time, irrevocable. About this, he reflected (how, it is true, reflect on it, reflecting it, restoring a certain flexibility to it?). Irrevocability would be the trait by which the void of the past marks, by giving them as impossible to relive and as thus already having been lived in an unsituable present, the appearances of events that are there only to cover over the void, to enchant it in hiding it, while all the same announcing it through the mark of irreversibility. The irrevocable is thus by no means, or not only, the fact that that which has taken place has taken place forever: it is perhaps the means—strange, I admit—for the past to warn us (preparing us) that it is empty and that the falling due—the infinite fall, fragile—that it designates, this infinitely deep pit into which, if there were any, events would fall one by one, signifies only the void of the pit, the depth of what is without bottom. It is irrevocable, indelible, yes: ineffacable, but because nothing is inscribed in it.

Irrevocability would be the slip that, by vertigo, in an instant, at the farthest remove from the present, in the absolute of the non-present, makes what "just happened" fall.

What has just taken place, would slip and would fall right away (nothing more rapid) through irrevocability, into "the terrifyingly ancient", there where nothing was ever present. Irrevocability would be, in this view, the slip or the fragile fall that abolishes time in time, effaces the difference between the near and the far, the marks of reference, the so-called temporal measures (all that makes contemporary) and shrouds everything in non-time, from which nothing could come back, less because there is no return than because nothing falls there, except the illusion of falling there.

◆    Let us admit that events are only "real" in the past, machine functioning in such a way that we could bring to mind, by a well-fitted memory, although with a slight doubt, all that the future could promise us or make us fear. But isn't the past always less rich than the future, and always other than it? Certainly, except if, the past being the infinitely empty and the future the infinitely empty, these were only the oblique way (the screen otherwise inclined) in which the void gives itself, imitating the possible-impossible, or the irrevocable-completed; or except if the law of the Eternal Return left no choice but to live the future in the past, the past in the future, without, however, the past and the future being summoned to change places according to the circulation of the Same since, between them, the interruption, the lack of presence, would prevent any communication other than by the interruption: the interruption lived either as the completed of the past or the possible of the future, or precisely as the incredible utopia of the Eternal Return. One cannot believe in the Eternal Return. This is its only guarantee, its "verification". Such is, there, the demand of the Law.

14

◆   If, in the "terrifyingly ancient", nothing was ever present, and if, having barely produced itself, the event, by the absolute fall, fragile, at once falls into it, as the mark of irrevocability announces to us, it is because (whence our cold presentiment) the event that we thought we had lived was itself never in a relation of presence to us nor to anything whatsoever.


◆   *The void of the future: there death has our future. The void of the past: there death has its tomb.*


◆   *In a certain way,* the law of the return—the Eternal Return of the Same—as soon as one has approached it by the movement that comes from it and that would be the time of writing if one did not have to say, also and at first, that writing holds the demand of the return, this law—outside the law—would lead us to take on (to undergo by way of the most passive passivity, the step/not beyond) the temporality of time, in such a way that this temporality, suspending, or making disappear, every present and all presence, would make disappear, or would suspend, the authority or the foundation from which it announces itself. The revelation of Surledj, revealing that everything comes again, makes the present the abyss where no presence has ever taken place and where the "everything comes again" has always already ruined itself. The law strikes the present with muteness, and, by way of the present, the present to come that the ordinary future—future present—accommodates itself to being. In such a way that: in the future will return what could not be present (the poetic mode), in the same way that in the past only what of the past never belonged to a present comes again (the narrative mode).


◆   On the one hand, "everything comes again" no longer allows this rythmic scansion that tightens the relation to time that is time itself in its temporality: time is every time "all" time, at "the same" time, without "all" and "the same" being able to maintain their directing power; past, present, future, these would be "all one", if it were not precisely unity that, in foundering, had not also modified the distinctions in turning them over to naked difference. That first. But on the other hand, "everything comes again" is not controlled by the shining in all directions that an eternal present, become the common place of space, would let us conceive. *Everything comes again,* signifying "everything will come again, everything already and forever has come again, on condition that it is not and has never been present", excludes "everything comes again" even in the form of a "nothing will come again".

◆     The demand of the return would then be the demand of a time without present, time that would also be that of writing, future time, past time, that the radical disjunction (in the absence of any present) of one from the other, even if they are the same, prevents us from identifying other than as the difference that repetition carries.

Between past, future, the greatest difference is given in that the one would repeat the other without the common measure of a present: as if between past and future the absence of present ruled in the simplified form of forgetfulness.

What will come again? Everything, *save* the present, the possibility of a presence.

◆     *"You will come again."—"I will come again."—"You won't come again."—"When you speak like that, I understand what it means: I'm here by way of the return, I'm thus not here: and I understand that this would be in the past, in a time so ancient that there has never been a present to correspond to it, that you have been here."—"But I am here, you see that."— "Yes, he said seriously, I'm here on condition that I forget that I'm here, remembering it one time, forgetting it another time, and just the same letting memory, forgetfulness, unfold them-*

selves, close themselves back up, without anyone who remembers, who forgets."

◆     Effaced before being written. If the word trace can be admitted, it is as the mark that would indicate as erased what was, however, never traced. All our writing—for everyone and if it were ever writing of everyone—would be this: the anxious search for what was never written in the present, but in a past to come.

◆     *"I haven't seen you in a long time." He said this even if I had just seen him; and it was true that it took time, however small the room was—spacious, nevertheless—to reach him, going the length of one table, then another, and perhaps yet another, as if he had had to follow a narrow street crossing the city.*

◆     *"We'll love them."—"We love them already."—"They don't know that we do."—"We're lucky they don't."—"They know nothing about what we expect from them."—"They live in ignorance: this is what makes them so beautiful, so lively."—"They're frightening."—"We're frightening."—They were young, beautiful, lively: he accepted all these words, snares so innocent even phantoms could not have let themselves be caught in them, knowing as well that plenty of other words could have been pronounced without attracting them the more or reaching them in that which preserved them. The only danger, danger of innocence, came from this right to be several, right which, diverting them from being one or the other, risked giving them up gently to the call that they could only hear as several: together? "We won't see anything as beautiful as them."—"Is this the right term?"—"They'll be too beautiful for anyone to notice it."—"I don't think they'd like our arranging things in their place."—"This place that they don't occupy,*

*happily." Happiness was there, in fact: a happiness that pro-
tected them from everything. "They won't know it, only together
will they be beautiful."*


♦     *He caught himself—melancholy surprise—hoping,
fearing: at the limit of these two words.*


♦     (to die): a far off legend, an ancient word that evoked
nothing, if not the dreamy thought that there was an unknown modality of time. To arrive at presence, to die, two
equally enchanted expressions.


♦     *The kindness of his welcome was perhaps in these words
that he began to remember just after he had left him: "If, coming here, you were to find this little room—all the same, not so
little, due to the three steps that made it possible to go down
towards the part where he waited for him, murmuring in the
corner—if you found it empty finally, then you could be sure
that, far from having neglected you, I would have shown myself worthy of your friendship."—"But isn't it empty?"—"Not
completely, because we're here, and only as one can say of the
city that it's empty." It is perhaps ever since this day, and so as
not to expose him to such kindness, that he only rarely faced
the possibility of finding the room as it would have been if he
had not come there to greet the most silent of hosts.*


♦     A word twice a word, that is to say, mute, this word
gently lightened by that which strikes it with speechlessness,
would be a word too many that would not reverberate. (he/it)
has this dullness, although one could represent it, alternately
and equally awkwardly, either as a massive door, condemned
by the bolts that close it, that anyone could go around in order
to reach the infinite space whose access it opens while appear-

18

ing as its prohibition, or as who knows what transparency, what void of the universe where everything—and every word—could disappear, if transparency were not the most uncrossable of crossroads.

♦     *He realized that he had to bear the truth of a self (without changing it into anything other than the canonic abbreviation of a rule of identity), if he wanted to help it maintain itself in this transparency, as yet never crossed, which did not let him accept any designation other than that which had been chosen as if in play.*

♦     All words are adult. Only the space in which they reverberate—a space infinitely empty, like a garden where, even after the children have disappeared, their joyful cries continue to be heard—leads them back towards the perpetual death in which they seem to keep being born.

♦     The transparency that does not let itself be crossed and from which nonetheless no reflexion comes back, except as the mark of inflexibility.

♦     *He remembered the first steps, the first warnings, the first unforeseeable signs of friendship, the first temptations that he hardly noticed. "Where did you leave them? What are they looking for? What are you looking for?" No search, and the room—with the tables placed end to end—freed him from the desire to find anything. "The name that would fit . . . the book that has been opened . . . the streets where they walk . . ." It was a murmur, the deceiful entreaty. And all of a sudden: reflect. "I have reflected that we love the places in which something has happened."—"You mean, things that one could tell about, could remember."—"We're not that demanding:*

*something."—"Something that would reduce or enhance the feeling of boredom."—"We're not bored."—"We're not capable of it."*

♦    (he/it) the hidden opening: this was what the name that was barely a word indicated and that designated him so eminently in designating nobody and that, by an indirect indication, which nonetheless seemed to relate itself more and more indirectly to this precise point, determined-undetermined, a void of the universe. Forbidden opening; on condition that one understand that it was and was not the prohibition—in whatever form—that would release the infinite possibility of opening.

The most difficult thing: not to identify or arrest the (he/it) as if it were the same and always in the very place where one had decided to take hold of it. The fact that (he/it), even in the most simple sentence, is somewhat apart from the sentence, but rather in each empty moment that the articulation sets aside for its play, discharges it from the role of the subject that it seems to accept. (he/it) thus doubles itself in redoubling itself indefinitely: the subject he/it that has this function in launching the sentence, is like the alibi of another he/it, which would not play any role, would fill no function, except that of putting itself out of work in repeating itself invisibly in an infinite series that analysis tries to catch and to take hold of again, after the fact, each time. But for that it seems necessary that there had been, at one end of the chain, to give itself the task of figuring the rule of identity, a myself capable of being there only to say "I".

♦    *The desire to meet them was as familiar to him as the silence of the snow on the rooftops. But, by himself, he could not keep the desire alive.*

♦    It is as if he had written in the margin of a book that would be written only much later, at a time when books, long

20

since having disappeared, would evoke only a terrifyingly ancient past, as if without speech, without any speech but this murmuring voice of a terrifyingly ancient past.

♦     As if it had been necessary to respond to a demand so much the more marked that it demanded nothing but this infinite response.

♦     *In a certain way,* it is necessary that presence—absolute satisfaction—realize itself by the accomplishment of discourse in order for the Eternal Return to reveal, under the veil of forgetfulness, the demand of a completely different modality of affirmation. Nietzsche, certainly, can be born before Hegel, and when he is born, in fact, it is always before Hegel; from this comes what one is tempted to call his madness: the relationship necessarily premature, always anticipated, always not now, thus without anything that can assure it by founding it on an actuality—whether this be of now, of the past (original) or of the future (prophetic). When one is content to say that madness is a reason ahead of reason, one wrongs both madness and reason. Even the maxim: "they were mad so that we no longer had to be", which Nietzsche might have accepted, still supposes simple temporal relations, always unifiable and reconciliable in the conception of a time essentially unique, itself, in as much as it is thought, withdraws from its own becoming, since it is dependent on a grand system. In this light, he is crazy who is wise before being so, before the letter. But the *other* madness—that which has no name to enclose it—would be an infinitely multiple relation that, even if called temporal, would hide itself from all that would subject it to time, even as outside of time. Madness is called so only by the language of the Law which, at best, assigns it the role of that which would precede it, that which would always be before the law, although the law in itself implies the impossibility of anything that could be anterior to it. That is why there is not madness, but there *will be* madness, the existence of this as a real possibility always having to be put in parentheses and under a conditional without condition. Which "madness" admits as well, since the parenthesis is its madness in which it would like to put everything, including itself.

♦ Nietzsche (if his name serves to name the law of the Eternal Return) and Hegel (if his name invites us to think presence as all and the all as presence) allow us to sketch a mythology: Nietzsche can only come after Hegel, but it is always before and always after Hegel that he comes and comes again. Before: since, even if it is thought as the absolute, presence has never gathered in itself the realized totality of knowledge; presence knows itself to be absolute, but its knowledge remains a relative knowledge, because it has not realized itself practically, and thus it knows itself only as a present unsatisfied practically, unreconciled with presence as all; thus, is not Hegel only a pseudo-Hegel? And Nietzsche always comes after, because the law he brings supposes the completion of time as present and in this completion its absolute destruction, such that the Eternal Return, affirming the future and the past as the only temporal authorities, authorities identical and unrelated, freeing the future of any present and the past of any presence, shatters thought up to this infinite affirmation: in the future will return infinitely what could in no form and never be present, in the same way that in the past that which, in the past, never belonged in any form to the present, has returned. There, from that point on, for Nietzsche, the demand to live and to think. And writing alone can respond to the demand, on condition that discourse as logos having realized itself, takes away any foundation on which writing could declare itself or support itself and exposes it to the threat, to the vain glamour, of what no one henceforth would dare name: mad writing.

♦ The madness of the *"everything comes again"*: it has a first simple trait, carrying within it the extravagance of forms

22

or of relations that exclude one another. It formulates in Hegelian language what can only destroy this language; this formulation is not, however, an accidental anachronism; the anachronism is its necessity: the "ideological delay" is its just hour; just as it could destroy only what realizes itself in it and completes itself in it and by the rigor of the completion that destroys it itself. *"Everything comes again"*: this is the logos of totality; for "everything" to come again, totality must have received from discourse and from practice its meaning and the realization of its meaning. And the present must be the unique temporal instance for the totality of presence and as presence to affirm itself. But "everything comes again" determines that the infinite of the return could not take the form of the circularity of the all and determines that no return could affirm itself in the present (whether this present is future or is a past present), that is, could not affirm itself except by the exclusion of any possibility and experience of a presence or by the affirmation of a time without present; a time without present would bear the weight of this exclusion, freed from any affirmation. The thought of the *everything comes again* thinks time in destroying it, but, by this destruction that seems to reduce it to two temporal instances, thinks it as infinite, infinity of rupture or interruption substituting an infinite absence for present eternity.

Saying that, we say almost nothing. We do not have the language to affirm the return by way of the detoured demand that would come to us from it, and language fell apart in Nietzsche, when he, with a mortal desire, desired to carry it to the impossible affirmation.


♦ *To awaken his attention: there was nothing to that; he was always awakened to the point that all that seemed to remain of him was the emptiness of a vigilant wait, the distracted absence, nonetheless, of inattention.*


♦ *The hope of transgressing the law was tied to the deception that, in this very movement of transgression, led him to*

*pose an equal law, although of a higher power, which he then
had to transgress anew, without any hope of being able to do so
except by posing a new and always higher law, which made of
this infinite passage from the law to its transgression and from
this transgression to another law the only infraction that up-
held the eternity of his desire.*

♦     Luck and grace, in being compared, help to determine
certain relations to the law. Grace is unjust, an unjustified
gift that does not take what is right into consideration, while
confirming it nonetheless. The law, without grace, would be
impossible to respect, that is, to maintain, even at a distance.
But the law, in its always absolute demand and by the limit
that it determines and that determines it, does not allow a
gracious rescue to intervene and make possible its impossible
observance. The law is empty authority, before which no one
in particular can maintain himself and which could not be
softened by mediation, the veil of grace that would make its
approach tolerable.

The law cannot transgress itself, since it exists only in
regard to its transgression-infraction and through the rupture
that this transgression-infraction believes it produces, while
the infraction only justifies, renders just what it breaks or
defies. The circle of the law is this: there must be a crossing in
order for there to be a limit, but only the limit, in as much as
uncrossable, summons to cross, affirms the desire (the false
step) that has always already, through an unforeseeable
movement, crossed the line. The prohibition constitutes itself
only by the desire that would desire only in view of the prohibition. And desire is the prohibition that frees itself in desiring itself, no longer as desire itself forbidden, but as desire (for
the) forbidden, which takes on the brilliance, the amiability,
the *grace* of the desirable, even if it is mortal. The law reveals
itself for what it is: less the command that has death as its
sanction, than death itself wearing the face of the law, this
death that desire (against the law), far from turning itself
away from it, gives itself as its ultimate aim, desiring until

24

death, in order that death, even as death of desire, is still the desired death, that which carries desire, as desire freezes death. The law kills. Death is always the horizon of the law: if you do this, you will die. It kills whoever does not observe it, and to observe it is also already to die, to die to all possibilities, but as its observance is nevertheless—if the law is Law—impossible and, in any case, always uncertain, always unrealized, death remains the unique falling due that only the love of death can turn away, for he who loves death makes the law vain in making it lovable. Such would be the detour of grace.

Grace does not save from death, but it effaces the mortal condemnation in making of the *saltus mortalis*—the bound without discretion and without precaution—the careless motion that concerns itself neither with condemnation nor with salvation, being the gift that has no weight and that is not weighed, gift of lightness, gift always light.

But isn't grace always the gift made by someone, gift unique and from the Unique? Would it not be characteristic of it to be grace only through the memory of its origin, through the always personal and always revocable relation, lived as fleeting and happy, with the power to give? Grace would be gracious only in this movement in which sovereignty grants itself by lovingly reminding of and recalling to the one who grants it. In this way it is different from the law. Because the law, even given as the gift *par excellence* (the gift of the Tables), affirms itself as law and without reference to anything higher: to it alone, pure transcendence. This is why it does not authorize any questions about it or beyond it, it awaits only answers, answers precise, sober, austere, not mechanical, but reflected on, studied, made always more right by study, patience, obedience without end. The law, law unique and from the Unique—is law only in the forgetting of its origin and by a demand that is proper to it, although it tends to have no other exteriority than itself: in this sense it is anonymous, designating the source from which it would have sprung only by the drying up which, at the limit, it represents.

The law says "in spite of you" [*"malgré toi"*] familiarity[3] that indicates no one. Grace says, "without you, without your being there for anything and in your own absence", but this familiarity which seems to designate only the lack of anyone, restores the intimacy and the singularity of the relation. Luck joins these two traits. Luck comes only through playing. And the game does not address itself to anyone in particular. He who is lucky is not lucky and is not so for himself or because of himself. The "without you" of luck frees, through the familiar address, for the anonymous.

◆    Luck is only another word for chance.[4] Good, bad, it is still luck and, always, good luck. Similarly for grace, which can be disgrace without renouncing the extreme good grace it owes to its "transcendence". "I am lucky" means then "I have chance" or, more correctly, there is between "me" and the necessity of a law this relation of prohibition that surely comes from the law, but has always already turned back on it to the point of prohibiting the law itself, provoking a kind of rupture. Prohibition strikes the law. This is a scandalous event. The law strikes itself with prohibition and, thus, in the most deceitful way (the august deceit of the law), restores another law, higher, that is, more other, in a more decisive relation with otherness, from which the prohibition is then supposed to come. Chance—either luck or grace that puts the law in parentheses, according to the time outside of time—is then reintroduced under the jurisdiction of another law, until, in its turn, this one—then, in its turn . . . It remains to determine in what relation neither lawful nor fortuitous would be the movement that would always pose an *other* law starting from the transgression, as from the law and as its other— transgression—movement of otherness, without law, without chance, movement that we in no way name by the negative of these words.

"I am lucky." Formula as strong as it is bold, since luck dispossesses and disappropriates. That which, oh gambler who pretends to speak in the name of the game, would end up saying: I possess what dispossesses, being the relation of dispossession. Which is to say that there is no luck for luck, and that the only luck would be in this anonymous relation that itself could not be called luck, or only this luck that does not fall due, with which the neuter would play in letting itself play in it.

◆ Transcendence, transgression: names too close to one another not to make us distrustful of them. Would transgression not be a less compromising way to name "transcendence" in seeming to distance it from its theological meaning? Whether it is moral, logical, philosophical, does not transgression continue to make allusion to what remains sacred both in the thought of the limit and in this demarcation, impossible to think, which would introduce the never and always accomplished crossing of the limit into every thought. Even the notion of the cut in its strictly epistemological rigor makes it easier to compromise, allowing for the possibility of overstepping (or of rupturing) that we are always ready to let ourselves be granted, even if only as a metaphor.

◆ It is not only with the law that luck has a remarkable relationship. With desire, it has and does not have the same relation of ambiguity. On the one hand, that should not surprise us, since, sometimes and at the same time, the law pretends that there would be desire only in the space of the game, where it attracts it by the stake and the prohibition, and, sometimes and at the same time, desire pretends to make the law its game or the game its own law or again to make the law only the product of an absence or abatement of desire. (Which again leads to this question: would desire not always already be its own lack, the void itself that makes it infinite, lack without lack?). But, on the other hand, luck and desire are far from being able to take one another's place. Desire is always ready to affirm that there is no luck but by desire and that desire is the only luck: which conforms to the "law" of desire and to what is left of the law in desire—the non-desiring. As for luck, even if it does not renounce its relation with the mortally desiring passion, it is only to affirm it in another way: desire must desire luck, it is thus that it is pure desire.

Luck plays with us, however, through that which names it, except if, in the same movement, we "succeed" in playing with it. When one *writes:* "To write is to seek luck", the one who writes braves, with the inappropriateness that is appropriate here, all the vigor of uncontrolled oppositions; because one must first write this and thus establish, with the proposition opened by the affirmation of writing, an already hidden relation with luck; and as luck is what cannot be sought, to write is to make of the search not the movement that would lead to luck, but rather luck's stake—this closed unclosed circle of the game in which lawless luck rules—rules, nevertheless, with the strict, regulated rigor that delimits the space where writing plays, when, seeking luck, it never attains it otherwise than as that which, in its turn, seeks writing in order to be luck.

To write is to seek luck, and luck is the search for writing, if it is only luck by the mark that, in advance, invisibly, responds to the line of demarcation—the interval of irregularity where luck-bad luck, game-law, are *separated* by the nil or infinite cesura and at the same time *exchanged,* but without a relation of reciprocity, of symmetry, nor even of a standard.

Luck is in search of writing, let's not forget it, and let's not forget that what it finds in the form of writing is, "luckily", bad luck, the fall of the dice thrown endlessly to fall again only once (and in this unique instance scratching out the unity, the totality, of the throws), since it is in falling and only in falling that they set the score.

Luck is the name by which chance attracts you so that you are not conscious of the unqualifiable multiplicity in which it loses you and with no other rules than those that always raise the multiple as a game: game of the multiple. Game whose stake it is, in suppressing that which divides into luck and bad luck, to raise the plurality endlessly. To play is thus always to play against luck and bad luck—binary logic—for the plurality of the game. But play? yes, play, even if you cannot. To play is to desire, to desire without desire, and already to desire to play.

◆     *The question he did not ask him. "What would you do if you were alone?"—"Well, the question wouldn't be asked."— "You mean there'd be no one to ask it."—"And no one to answer it."—"There'd be no time for that."*


◆     For there to be a play of questions and answers, time must keep its unitary structure with its three variables. The predominance of the present as thought and as life (the intemporal present and presence to oneself in the living distant) is perhaps all the more marked by the near impossibility of not relating past and future to an actuality that has become or is to come; that is, of not thinking one and the other as a present that has fallen due or will fall due. The accomplishment of history would be this taking back, in a present henceforth actual, of any historical possibility: being always thinks itself and speaks itself in the present. When the affirmation of the Eternal Return of the Same imposes itself on Nietzsche, in the revelation that overwhelms him, it seems at first that it privileges, in giving it the colors of the past and the colors of the future, the temporal demand of the present: what I live today opens time to the depths, giving it to me in this unique present as the double infinity that would come to reunify itself in the present; if I have lived it an infinite number of times, if I am called upon to relive it an infinite number of times, I am there at my table for eternity and to write it eternally: all is present in this unique instant that repeats itself, and there is nothing but this repetition of Being in its Same. But Nietzsche came very quickly to the thought that there was no one at his table, neither present in the Being of the Same, nor Being in its repetition. The affirmation of the Eternal Return had provoked either temporal ruin, leaving nothing else to think but dispersion as thought (the open-eyed silence of the prostrate man in a white shirt), or, perhaps even more decisive, the ruin of the present alone, henceforth stricken with prohibition and, with it, the unitary root of the whole torn out. As if the repetition of the Return had no other function than to put in parentheses, in putting the present in parentheses, the number 1 or the word Being, compelling thereby an alteration that neither our language nor our logic can admit. For even if we dared to designate the past conventionally in numbering it 0 and the future in number it 2, while postulating the suppression, with the present, of any unity, we would still have to mark the equal power of the 0 and the 2 in the unmarked and unmeasurable distance of their difference (such as the demand by which the future and the past would affirm themselves as the same supposes it, if, in the catastrophe of the Eternal Return, it were not precisely any common denominator or numerator that had disappeared with the form of the present) and to mark that this equal power would not allow us to identify them, nor even to think them together, but not to exclude them from one another either, since the Eternal Return says also that one would be the other, if the unity of Being had not, by an inadmissible interruption, in fact ceased to order the relations.

♦    The past was written, the future will be read. This could be expressed in this form: what was written in the past will be read in the future, without any relation of presence being able to establish itself *between* writing and reading.

♦    *"I can do no better than to entrust myself to your loyalty."—"You do better, nevertheless, and rightly, because even if I am loyal, how would we put up with a loyalty without law?"*

♦    *I am not master of language. I listen to it only in its effacement, effacing myself in it, towards this silent limit where it waits for one to lead it back in order to speak, there where presence fails as it fails there where desire carries it.*

♦    A speech without presence, the perpetuity of dying, the death of eternity from which the church song appeals

30

forcefully to free us, recognizing in it the space of speech always deprived of God, that is, freed from presence.

♦ Let us think of the obscure combat between language and presence, always lost by one and by the other, but all the same won by presence, even if this be only as presence of language. Even if speech, in its perpetual disappearance, carries death, the void, absence, it always resuscitates with it what it cancels or suspends, including at this limit where it itself disappears, whether it does not succeed in exhausting presence, or whether, exhausting it, it must then, through negation, affirm itself anew as presence of speech that thus vainly exhausts presence. Perhaps here only he who does not fight wins. It is because it accepts language that presence affirms itself in it, making it accessory and propitious, exalting it to the point of opening it from top to bottom, so that it coincides with the opening that is presence. It is thus also in struggling for presence (in accepting to make itself naively the memorial of something that presents itself in it) that language treacherously destroys it. This happens by way of writing. In appearance, writing is there only to conserve. Writing marks and leave marks. What is entrusted to it remains. With it history starts in the institutional form of the Book and time as inscription in the heaven of stars begins with earthly traces, monuments, works. Writing is remembrance, written remembrance prolongs life during death.

But what remains of presence when it has to hold on to itself only this language in which it extinguishes itself, fixes itself? Maybe only this question. It is not certain that presence maintained by writing as writing is not completely foreign to "true", "living" presence, that which is in fact always the source of presence, truth of presence, vision of presence. The only relation that writing would then maintain with presence would be Meaning, relation of light, relation that the demand to write tends precisely to rupture in no longer submitting itself to the sign.

The defeat that writing would seem to inflict on presence in making it no longer presence, but subsistence or substance, is a defeat for itself. From this point of view, writing alienates presence (and alienates itself). An instrument, and, as such, a bad instrument; serving to communicate, even if it communicates imperfectly. And if presence alienates itself in it, it is because, even in the expression from which it does not set itself free and that encloses it, it maintains its right to declare itself without expressing itself. That would be enough for its triumph.

♦     Writing, the demand to write, does not struggle *against* presence in favor of absence, nor *for* it in pretending to preserve it or communicate it. Writing is not accomplished in the present, nor does it present, nor does it present itself: still less does it represent, except to play with the repetitive that introduces into the game the temporally ungraspable anteriority of the beginning again in relation to any power to begin, as if the re-present, without anticipating a presence yet to come, without assigning it to the past either, in the excessive multiplicity that the word indicates, played with a plurality always supposed by the return. To write in this sense, is always first to rewrite, and to rewrite does not refer to any previous writing, any more than to an anteriority of speech or of presence or of signification. Rewriting, doubling which always precedes unity or suspends it in unmarking it: rewriting holds itself apart from any productive initiative and does not claim to produce *anything*, not even the past or the future or the present of writing. Rewriting in repeating what does not take place, will not take place, has not taken place, inscribes itself in a non-unified system of relations that cross paths without any point of crossing affirming their coincidence, inscribing itself under the demand of the return by which we are torn from the modes of temporality that are always measured by a unity of presence.

Rewriting is a surplus, the supplementary relation which, at the limit, could not define itself by anything in regard to which it would add itself—excess of nothing and still excessive. Thus all considerations of influence, of causality, of model, of makes and counterfeits are rendered vain—except in that "plagiarism" such as Lautréamont's irony proposes it to us, could not come after a text given as initial, even to initiate it to itself, but would repeat it as unwritten or would repeat the text about which there is no way to know if it had been produced before, since it is always and in advance reproduced.

The "re" of the return inscribes like the "ex", opening of every exteriority: as if the return, far from putting an end to it, marked the exile, the beginning in its rebeginning of the exodus. To come again would be to come to ex-center oneself anew, to wander. Only the *nomadic* affirmation *remains*.

♦    *"Always, I come again."—"In as much as you find in yourself the ability to remain at the furthest remove."—"It is only here that I would find the distant."*

♦    *"Already I see you come, coming back slowly, there among others who help us with their solitude."*

♦    *Was there still an obstacle that he could not get past to reach the immense uncertain space, or did this obscure and devastated space (serial desert) constitute the only impediment, the last obstacle?*

♦    *The voice without voice, a murmur that he did not know, hearing it no longer, if he still heard it, sometimes a vibration so sharp that he was sure of it—was the grating tracing of the chalk on the slate.*

♦    *What they know, they know from us. And what we know is for no one or for nothing.*

♦    In the view of the demand to write, in the multiplicity in which it disseminates itself, nothing is either friendly nor sacred, events are useless, days unsanctified, men neither divine nor human. Those who carry this demand are transported by it and disappear in it: even if their name then serves to name it, they are neither important nor great. In their disparate plurality, even though they belong to the multiple and are real only as multiple, they remain strangers, separate from one another, crossing paths without meeting: this is their solitude, a plurality that constitutes them neither out of their own singularity nor in view of a superior unity.

Should the demand to write seek itself in the existence of those who seem to consecrate themselves to it: there is no biography for writing. Should it seek itself in works: these, closed in their magnificence, pretend to shine only for themselves whose central secret accepts no translation, while, open, works have always already let pass the act of writing that goes through them, using these works only to fill them momentarily. Or again, letting itself be affirmed in a more general knowledge, the knowledge proper to the necessity of marks, of inscriptions, of gestures, even of traces, knowledge by which it would end up judging scientific ideology or even giving its opinion on the ability of the sciences to attain a certain scientificity. In doing this, it risks immersing itself in a badly defined problematic that eternal metaphysics has no difficulty taking up in introducing it into the hopeful confidence of its books. What then to do with this movement that does not recognize itself in anything it does not contest? Perhaps maintain it as a demand always previously exhausted, that is, as non-living repetition, forgetting that there is no time for writing, if writing has always preceded itself in the form of a rewriting.

♦     Friendship for the demand to write that excludes all friendship.

♦     The anonymous after the name is not the nameless anonymous. The anonymous does not consist in refusing the name in withdrawing from it. The anonymous puts the name in place, leaves it empty, as if the name were there only to let itself be passed through because the name does not name, but is the non-unity and non-presence of the nameless. (he/it), which does not designate anything, but awaits what forgets itself in it, helps to question this demand of the anonymous. Would it be enough, however, to say that (he/it), without having value or meaning in itself, would allow whatever inscribes itself in it to affirm itself in a determination that is different every time? Or again, to attribute to it the function of an "analogon", a mode of absence in which every image would be caught, the void of a symbol, always ready to fill itself with diverse possible meanings and always in default? (he/it) is not such that it would only receive the indetermination of its proper meaning in letting itself be determined by all that would be said beyond it, through it (even though the word being is perhaps lit by the light of the meaning that rises up when it is pronounced, only if something that is, would be or would not be—this happens all the time, but could just as well not happen—comes face to face with itself in language and then obscures it and covers it up without covering it.) (he/it) welcomes the enigma of being without being's being able to lessen its own enigma. (he/it) pronounces itself without there being a position or deposition of existence, without presence or absence affirming it, without the unity of the word coming to dislodge it from the between-the-two in which it disseminates itself. (he/it) is not "that one", but the neuter that marks it (as (he/it) appeals to the neuter), leads it back towards the displacement without place that robs it of any grammatical place, a sort of lack in becoming between two, several or all words, thanks to which these interrupt each other, without which they would signify nothing, but which upsets them constantly to the very silence in which they extinguish themselves. The anonymous is borne by the (he/it) that always speaks the name forgotten in advance.

♦      We write to forget our name, wanting it, not wanting it, and we of course know that another we is necessarily given in return, but which is it? The collective sign that the anonymous addresses to us (since this new name—the same one—expresses nothing but nameless reading, never centered on some denominated reader, nor even on a unique possibility of reading). Thus, this name that we are proud of or unhappy with is then the mark of our belonging to the nameless from which nothing emerges: the public nothingness—inscription that effaces itself on an absent tomb.

♦    The vain struggle for the anonymous. Impersonality is not enough to guarantee the anonymous. The work, even if it is without author and always becoming in relation to itself, delimits a space that attracts names, a possibility of reading that is determined every time, a system of references, a theory that appropriates it, a meaning that clarifies it. Of course, we have dispensed with these (although again this is not sure) with the great names. At the same time that Nietzsche—again a very great name—lets us know that the work, that of the artist or of the philosopher, invents only after the fact he who, having created it, *must* have created it, we know that the work, in its historical necessity, is always modified, transformed, traversed, separated from itself, delivered to its outside, by all the works that seem to come only after it, according to a movement of recurrence whose model Hegel provided. We are not dupes of the present that would make us believe in an authority we have or in an influence we exercise, still less are we concerned with the past, still less presumptuous of a future. We penetrate the pretended impersonal responsibility of groups in which is affirmed, secretly or directly, the right of some to lead in aggrandizing their name with that of the group. The "cult of personality" does not begin with the person who places himself above others to incarnate a historical truth. It begins with this truth itself, whether it is that of the party, of the country, of the world, truth always ready, once it immobilizes itself, to unify itself in a name, a person, a people, an epoque. How then does one arrive at this anonymous whose only mode of approach is *haunting intimacy,* uncertain obsession that always dispossesses.

36

The exteriority that excludes every exterior and every interior, as it precedes their succeeding, ruining for them every beginning and every end, and in such a way that it hides itself in the revelation that represents it at once as law there where every law is failing, as return there where every arrival is lacking, as eternal Same when non-identity unmarks itself in it without continuity without interruption, as repetition there where nothing is counted: this is the "concept" (non-conceptualizable) that should help us to maintain ourselves, we the named, close to the inhospitable host who has always preceded us into our house or into our self, even though he has always withdrawn us from our best or most faulty intimacy to relate us, half complacent, half moribund, to this very relation that collapses into anonymous passion.

Let us be clear that we will never have gotten away from the name, even if we are marked by the pre-original anonymous. The anonymous is given to us in the name itself, not freeing us in any way from ourselves, from our identity and from this face that needs, to refuse itself to any access, the faceless, the gazeless, mask that transforms everything into a mask and that nothing unmasks. The more strong and justified the name, the more it gives hold to the perversion of the anonymous; the more that greatness, creative force, indubitable truth present themselves in a name, the more it is ready to denounce itself as the error or the injustice which has thrived at the expense of the nameless. But, in return, everything happens as if the anonymous, shadow of which light would be unaware that it shines only to project it, arranged the whole comedy of glories, of powers, of sanctities, in order to bring itself near to us, signalling to us across signification and precisely there where every sign would be lacking.

When we sign, affirming our identity, we become responsible well beyond this signature, to the point that this responsibility has forever put us aside, signing to disappropriate us, like a forgerer who would not try to pass as true, but would make the true shine out as false. The element in-signiates: that which can never appear alone and which the act of signing, of designating, of signifying, introduces as fraudulent, clandestine cold that never lets itself be taken by surprise, double anterior, shadow without light in that the shadow always makes use of some clarity to show itself or to hide itself, seeming thus to follow it.


◆    Do we approach the anonymous if we yield (supposing that there were enough passivity in us for such a concession) to the attraction of dying, indeed, of thought? If to think were to sink into nothingness, as we would think with happiness, with fright. But, sinking through thought, we are immediately carried to our highest possible.


◆    I think of the calling of the names in the camps. Naming carries the mortal play of the word. The arbitrariness of the name, the anonymous that precedes it or accompanies it, the impersonality of nomination bursts forth in the manner of *something terrible* in this situation in which language plays its murderous role. The proper name—a number—is disappropriated by the very power that designates it and by the power of interminable language. What does "proper name" signify here? Not the right to be there in person; on the contrary the terrifying obligation by which what would like to preserve itself in the name of a private unhappiness is drawn out into the public square, into the cold and the impoverishment of the outside, with nothing that can assure any refuge. The prohibition against having anything of one's own and against keeping anything having to do with oneself is pronounced by the proclaiming of the name or of that which holds its place. The call in the camps makes appear, certainly in a way that leaves no room for any decent camouflage, the meaning of any civil-state formality (as of any verification of identity, which gives place, in our refined civilizations, to all police violences and deprivations of liberty). Language does not communicate, it makes naked and according to nakedness—the placing outside—that is proper to it and that one can only temper, that is to say, pervert, by the detour which is the game of this always oblique outside, a game that is also and in

38

the first place a game of language without right or direction, indirect as through a *game*.

♦ *They appear disappearing, like in the multitude of likes: unique in as much as repeated. Without residence or town, they go, indiscernable among all. Marchers to infinity, if they leave no trace, in that you will recognize them without discovering them.*

♦ If it is true that there is (in the Chinese language) a written character that means both "man" and "two", it is easy to recognize in man he who is always himself and the other, the happy duality of dialogue and the possibility of communication. But it is less easy, more important perhaps, to think "man", that is to say, also "two", as separation that lacks unity, the leap from 0 to duality, the 1 thus giving itself as the forbidden, the between-the-two.

We can borrow this thought from Confucius, speaking of measure and mean: "Measure, mean, are the extremes of man." If the middle is the extreme, the center is never in the middle. Nobody who is in relation only to nobody keeps the measure.

To give words back their meaning? Not to give words back to meaning?

If, thinking the mean as just mean, we take advantage of this to exclude the extremes and to refuse the "last things" the right to be thought, then it is the mean that becomes the limit, and to think the measure is to think at the limit. Not to think the One is just the same to let oneself be led by the One to the edge of indifference.

♦ Not to write a line (like Socrates) is perhaps not to privilege speech, but to write by default and in advance, since, in this abstention, the space of writing in which Plato already works is prepared and is decided.

◆     To think the Eternal Return is to seduce thought in tempting it with the appearance of a tautology—the dream of the Same, the aridity of a logical identity, promise of a coherence that breaks down thus: the promise itself takes place in a language, while the coherence sought needs another language which, in its otherness, revokes the promise and ruins the speech that was supposed to fulfill it.

"A promise was made.—But already ruined by the speech that proposes it, since it promises, suspending any present, the impossibility of an ordinary future, appropriate to the order in which it could fulfill itself, could show itself as promise."

The formulation of the Eternal Return is necessarily made in another time than that in which it "would verify itself": in the language, ours, in which one must always speak of time as future, present, past, Nietzsche is mad each time he seeks to affirm his affirmation rigorously; but, in the silent language of his madness in which he seems to us to suffer the consequences of this passage to another language removed from the ordinary forms of temporality, he is still mad, mad in view of his madness itself taken as a "new reason" where he appears to us naively reconciled with the coherence of a thought, as if he were always lagging behind, by a madness, by a language, the language in which the formulation of the return has always already engaged him. Mad?—But of a madness other than ours, other than his.


◆     With Hegel, if, as he says, the concept is established as that to which nature could not be sufficient, how content oneself with the concept as absolute contentment? The Eternal Return marks the surplus that every mark of identity produces, without the mark of this surplus suspending identity, and without this surplus ever being, marked, free of the mark, acquitted by it.


◆     *"Here we are then once again."—"This is what we have rejoiced at saying every time and the first time."—"Every meet-*

*ing was already a meeting again for us."—"I understand that,
I would understand it better if I didn't know that it's always
too late for us to meet."—"Too late, it's true, because there is no
right moment."—"Did you hear the sound of their voice?"—"As
I don't even hear my own."—"Ah, they will always surprise
us."*

♦     *He enters, he speaks with the words that are already
there to welcome him, feeling an equal pain whether he speaks
or remains silent.*

♦     *"What I learned from them is that, already, before, they
were close to us, separated only by a little, perhaps only in that
they could not be late, at least not in any form of the present
that exists."—"They pass."—"They have always already
passed, but we don't miss them by much."—"We miss them all
the more."*

*"Nothing is important to them."—"I wouldn't say that, I
would say that it's importance that's not important to them."*

*There was, in this way of speaking, in presence through
speech, something true to which even silence was not sufficient
to respond, unless to open itself again onto silence.*

♦     The Eternal Return of the Same: the having been, repetition of a will take place as having been, does not signal any
presence, even that of old. The Eternal Return would say this,
it would say that in what has been, no present is retained,
except in this speaking of it, if it were spoken.

In this sense, the necessity of thinking what has been and
of coming after it without reference to presence has always—
apart from any proximity—put us far away as a distance from
any distancing. The far away that distends every mode of
absence, as of presence.

If one says, like Parmenides, "that has never been and will
never be because it is", one quickly frees the past and the

future of any present, since "it is" gives itself as never re-presenting itself in the "having been" or the "will be".

(Even in the law of the Eternal Return, the past could not repeat the future *as* the future would repeat the past. The repetition of the past as future frees for a completely different modality—which one could call prophetic. In the past, what is given as repetition of the future does not give the future as repetition of the past. Dissymmetry is at work in repetition itself. How then think dissymmetry in terms of the Eternal Return? That is what is perhaps most enigmatic.

♦ The fragmentary: what comes to us from it, question, demand, practical decision? To no longer be able to write except in relation to the fragmentary is not to write in frag-ments, unless the fragment is itself a sign for the fragmen-tary. To think the fragmentary, to think it in relation to the neuter, the two seeming to pronounce themselves together, without a community of presence and as outside one another. The fragmentary: writing belongs to the fragmentary when all has been said. There would have to have been exhaustion of the word and by the word, accomplishment of all (of presence as all) as logos, in order that fragmentary writing could let itself be re-marked. Still, we cannot, thus, writing, free our-selves from a logic of totality in considering it as ideally com-pleted, in order to maintain as "pure remainder" a possibility of writing, outside of everything, useless or endless, whose study a completely different logic (that of repetition, of limits, and of the return)—still difficult to disengage—claims to guarantee us. What is already decided is that such a writing would never be "pure", but, on the contrary, profoundly al-tered, with an alteration that could not be defined (arrested) in regard to a norm, not only because it always coexists with all forms of existence, of speech, of thought, of temporality, which alone would make it possible, but because it excludes the consideration of a pure form, excluding even an approach to itself as true or proper in its very disappropriation; even all the reversals which we easily use up—beginning again as

42

beginning, disappropriation as authenticity, repetition as difference—leave us within the logic of validity.

The fragmentary expresses itself best, perhaps, in a language that does not recognize it. Fragmentary: meaning neither the fragment, part of a whole, nor the fragmentary in itself. The aphorism, the proverb, maxim, citation, thoughts, themes—verbal cells in being further removed than the infinitely continuous discourse whose content is "its own continuity", continuity that is assured of itself only in giving itself as circular and, by this turn, submitting itself to the preliminary of a return whose law is outside, which outside is outside the law.

♦ *He followed them, uncertain that he did not push them in front of him, like great impassioned shades. Following them, following only the attraction he felt in common with them, attracted only toward the attraction. "Keep attacking us."—"Discourage us." He compares them to careless words, united by chance, mad, and mad to be together. "Never, before, did you use such a word."—"But what would this word be?"— "You know it."—"Then I wouldn't use it this time."—"It comes to us from them."—"Or they come to us from it."—"And it, from where would it come to us?"*

♦ *In a serious tone, as if to remind him that they were there without any right other than to use up this right in speaking, to use up the right to speech. "We are beyond being able to hold on for a long time."—"Yes, in the time to which we do not hold."—"But which gives us this hold in the form of a conversation."*[5]

♦ *"You are their moderator."—"In their immobility, they move about constantly."—"They represent such an insistence in such an absence of present that their reappearance could only be our own."*

43

*"Would they attach importance to our words?"—"The answer is beyond our power."—"But answer to what question, if not to that which goes beyond all powers, our own included."*

♦    The demand of the fragmentary, not being the sign of the limit as limitation of ourselves, nor of language in relation to life or of life in relation to language, offers itself nevertheless, hiding itself, as a play of limits, play that does not yet have any relation to any limitation. The demand of the fragmentary: play of limits in which no limitation plays; the fragmentary, a dissociation of limit and limitation, even though it marks a separation of the law, such that this separation is not taken back, included, in the law, the law that is understood, nevertheless, as a separation.

♦    *"What you propose would be a dangerous and even difficult undertaking, if indeed you were proposing it, but no more so than our having proposed to live without asking ourselves if we had the means necessary to do so—as soon as we ask it, they are lacking—, you didn't ask yourself if you had enough strength to see your venture, if it is one, through."—"I did ask myself and I ask myself constantly. And the answer: I don't have enough strength, I have enough emptiness for it."*

♦    Violence is at work in language, and, more decidedly, in the speech of writing, in as much as language conceals itself from work: this action of concealing itself again belongs to violence.

♦    Madness: let us suppose a language from which this word would be excluded, another in which it would be forgotten in relation to all the other words, another where the terrified search, forbidden, for this one word, lost and constantly

44

threatening, constantly interrogatory, would suffice, orienting all the possibilities of speech, to submit language to the only word that had deserted it. A supposition (mad, it is true), but also easy: on condition that we make use of a language in which madness would be given by a name. In general, we ask ourselves, by the intermediary of experienced practitioners, if such or such a man falls under the judgement of such a word. Strictly, we maintain this word in the interrogative position: Hölderlin was mad, but was he? Or else we hesitate to special-ize it, not only with scientific doubt, but in order not to, by making it precise, immobilize it in a certain knowledge: even schizophrenia, in evoking the madness of extremes, the dis-tance that distances us in advance from ourselves in separat-ing us from any power of identity, always says too much about it, or pretends to say too much about it. Madness would thus be a word in perpetual incongruance with itself and interroga-tive throughout, such that it would put into question its possi-bility and, through it, the possibility of the language that would admit it, thus would put interrogation itself into ques-tion, in as much as it belongs to the play of language. To say: Hölderlin is mad is to say: is he mad? But, it is, starting from there, to make madness so foreign to any affirmation that it could not find a language without putting it under the threat of madness: language, as such, gone mad. *Mad language* would be, in any speech, not only the possibility that would make it speak at the risk of making it non-speaking (risk without which it would not speak), but the limit that detains all language and which, never fixed in advance, nor the-oretically determinable, still less such that one could write: "there is a limit", thus outside of any "there is", could inscribe itself only on the basis of its own crossing—the crossing of the uncrossable—and, from this, prohibited. Whence (perhaps) the astonishment with which we are seized when we learn, learning it from Hölderlin and from Nietzsche, that the Greeks recognized in Dionysis the "mad god": expression that we make more familiar to ourselves in interpreting it: god who makes mad or madness that makes divine. But the "mad god"? How do we accept what comes to us by the force of such an irregularity? A god, not far away, responsible for some

45

general irregularity, but present, presence itself, in its revelatory suddeness: presence of the mad god? The mad god: presence of the outside that has always already suspended, forbidden, presence. Such is the riddle of the Eternal Return.


♦     That madness is present in every language is not enough to establish that it is not omitted in them. The name could elude it in that the name as name gives to the language that uses it for a peaceful communication the right to forget that with this word outside of words language's rupture with itself is introduced: rupture that only *another* language would allow to speak (without, however, communicating it).

But the madness that shatters language in leaving it apparently intact, leaves it intact only to accomplish in it its invisible destruction.


♦     To write is perhaps to not write in rewriting—to efface (in writing over) that which is not yet written and that rewriting not only covers over, but restores obliquely in covering it over, in making us think that there was something before, a first version (a detour) or, worse, an original text, engaging us thus in the process of the illusion of infinite deciphering.


♦     Speech is always the speech of authority (to speak is always to speak according to the authority of speech). But there is no sceptre for the one who writes, even disguised as a beggar's stick: nothing to lean on and no moving along.


♦     "The ever alluring secret of life is that life, which is for all of us without secrets and which has taken away all possibilities, remains alluring.—By its mortal limit.—By the limit of which one does not know if life would not be death's limit. So that in living we would know the extreme limit of death, on condition that we go through life—the crossings of life—in an unlimited way, with mortal desire.—Yes, it is indeed that; we are in relation, in life and through the desire to live, to the limit that death, without succeeding, pretends to break. Life would be the forbidden of death: forbidden to death? except in that the forbidden would be death itself."


◆     *"Let's not speak about them too much. It's about us that we might end up speaking."—"Knowing them, through ourselves, better than we know ourselves, even if we know ourselves in every way."*


◆     To say, to say according to what there is to say, implies a distance that we cannot interpret temporally, even if it is prepared in a sort of passive future, and it is also to say again according to the already spoken formula, thus to demand the impossible coexistence of past and future as such: or to involve oneself in the affirmation of the return.

The separation put to work in the act of writing: how much passivity, how much worklessness are needed to respect it, and, doing so, to betray it. In the ethical obligation, in the demand of the historical struggle, in the eschatological affirmation, nothing allows one to decide if the altered manner in which the distance seems to propose itself does not restore it to the demand that excludes it from any affirmation, pure or impure. Yes, why would "morality" not be the silence that imposes itself in any speech—what is obligatory in it—such that every speech would be moral, but always impossible to get hold of in morality (lost by it, which cannot say anything about itself), escaping it in remaining unknown to it?


◆     *"Even though there is no reason for you to come here, it seems that every time you come, you have an extraordinary reason to come."*

♦    The name of God signifies not only that what is named by this name would not belong to the language in which this name occurs, but that this name, in a way that is difficult to determine, would no longer be a part of this language, even apart from it. The idolatry of the name or only the reverence that makes it unpronouncable (sacred) is related to this disappearance of the *name* that the name itself makes appear and that makes us give more importance to the language in which it makes itself obscure, to the point of giving it as forbidden. Far from raising us to lofty significations, all those that theology authorizes, it does not give place to anything that is proper to it: pure name that does not name, but is rather always to be named, the name as name, but, in that, hardly a name, without nominative power, attached as if by chance to language and, thus, transmitting to it the power—a devastating one—of non-designation, that relates it to itself.

God: language speaks only as the sickness of language in as much as it is fissured, burst open, separated, failure that language recuperates immediately as its validity, its power and its health; recuperation that is its most intimate malady, of which God, name always irrecuperable, who is always to be named and never names anything, seeks to cure us, a cure in itself incurable.


♦    *Between them, the fear, the fear shared in common, and, through the fear, the abyss of fear over which they join one another without being able to do so, dying, each alone, of fear.*


♦    If, in order to deny, it is necessary to speak, and speaking, to affirm; if, consequently, language seems not to be able to free itself from a first affirmation, so that, once you speak, you are already the prisoner, always belatedly struggling against it, of an enunciation that affirms itself in speech, one would still have to know what this affirmation, enunciation, means. Does it only say what is (*the sky is blue*)? Or, in saying *the sky is blue* does it say: before enunciating and in enunciating, I have transgressed the silent prohibition in turning it into a positive prescription, speaking then according to what there is to say (the must-say). Yes, something always precedes us when we speak: the very separation that is nothing positive or enunciative, that would be rather the distance of the saying-between that we know only, having already fixed it, as prohibition. The must-say of the trangression (which is not a negation either, the simple refusal of a limitation), this is what, seeming to speak in every speech, makes it weighty to the point of silencing it.

Speaking is, forcing oneself to speak, to speak the obligation of the must-say (the right to speech, right without right) that pronounces itself facing the prohibition.

◆    *Each knowing that the other was going to die, every-thing was enlarged by a generosity of space. Nocturnal provocation, when wakefulness is not preoccupied with time.*

◆    The fragmentary. There is no experience of it, in the sense that one does not admit it in any form of present, that it would remain without subject if it took place, thus excluding every present and all presence, as it would be excluded from them. Fragments, marks of the fragmentary, referring to the fragmentary that refers to nothing and has no proper reference, nevertheless attesting to it, pieces that do not compose themselves, are not part of any whole, except to make fragmentary, not separated or isolated, always, on the contrary, effects of separation, separation always separated, the passion of the fragmentary effects of effects.

◆    *As if a feeling independent from them were coming from them.*

49

◆    Writing is not destined to leave traces, but to erase, by traces, all traces, to disappear in the fragmentary space of writing, more definitively than one disappears in the tomb, or again, to destroy, to destroy invisibly, without the uproar of destruction.

Writing according to the fragmentary invisibly destroys surface and depth, real and possible, above and below, manifest and hidden. There is then no hidden discourse that an apparent discourse would preserve, not even an open plurality of significations awaiting interpretive reading. To write at the level of the incessant murmur is to expose oneself to the decision of a lack that marks itself only by a surplus without place, impossible to put in place, to distribute in the space of thoughts, words and books. To respond to this demand of writing is not only to oppose a lack to a lack or to play with the void to procure some privative effect, nor is it only to maintain or indicate a blank between two or several affirmative enunciations; what then? perhaps first to carry a space of language to the limit from which the irregularity of another speaking, nonspeaking, space comes back, which effaces it or interrupts it and which one approaches only through its alterity, marked by the effect of effacement.


◆    *Free me from the too long speech.*


◆    The fragmentary not being experience, not being form or subject of writing, not being another order in comparison to the order of the book, even as passage to a disorder; still, obscure demand under the attraction of which the space of writing gives place to marks or points of singularity through which pass multiple (irregular) lines that make the points disappear as unique even in maintaining them in a position of singularity, so that a quasi-infinite multiplicity of crossings can repeat itself in it, without the repetition supressing the mark of singularity nor dissolving this in identity. It is as if this space were given as correlative or supplementary or even secondary (in this sense inessential), even in repelling, in bursting open, that of which it would seem to be the correlate or supplement, secondary then without any priority. Whence the work of obscurity that the beginning again conducts and conducts always more obscurely. Reading, writing are exchanged in favor of this "correlate" that they struggle to prevent, struggling also against the power in them to produce it or to restore it.

It is not a matter of substituting reading for writing or of privileging one over the other, but of redoubling them so that the law of one is the prohibition of the other. Through the fragmentary, writing and reading change functions. As long as writing is writing a book, this book is either completed or maintained by reading, or threatened by that which tends to reduce it or alter it, even though it is always and again, by its essence, supposed to be undamaged in the unreal totality (the work, the masterpiece) that it has once and for all constituted. But if to write is to arrange marks of singularity (fragments) from which routes can indicate themselves without reuniting nor joining the marks, but as their separating—separating of a space of which we know only the separation: the separation, without knowing from what it separates—there is always a risk that reading, instead of animating the multiplicity of crossing routes, reconstitutes a new totality from them, or, worse, seeks, in the world of presence and of sense, to what reality or thing to complete correspond the voids of this space given as complementary, but complementary of nothing.

♦   Characters: they are in the position of characters, and still these are points of singularity (local or site specific fires), immobile, although the route of a movement in a rarified space, in the sense that almost nothing can happen in it, traces itself from these to others, multiple routes by which, fixed, they do not cease to change places, nor, identical, to change. Rarified space, which the effect of rarity tends to make infinite to the very *limit* that does not bind it. The effect of rarity is proper to the fragmentary. Death here, far from making a work, has already done its work: mortal workless-ness. Through this, writing according to the fragmentary, al-ways taking place there where there is a place of dying and thus as according to perpetual death, brings on the scene, on a base of absence, semblances of sentences, remainders of lan-guage, imitations of thought, simulations of being. Lie that no truth upholds, forgetting that supposes nothing forgotten and that is detached from every memory: with no certainties, ever.

Desire turned back into desire. Like a collision of lights.


◆　*Meanwhile, between them and us, there is a relation of fraternity, close to one another to the point of living only when exposed to dying for one another, as in a reciprocal suicide in which one would prolong his life so that the other dies in it more gently, that we are called upon to maintain ourselves up until the end.*


◆　*Fraternity: we love them, we can do nothing for them, if not help them to reach the threshold.*

The threshold, what indiscretion and weight there would be in speaking of it as if it were death. In a certain way, and forever, we have known that death was only a metaphor to help us crudely represent the idea of a limit to ourselves, while the limit excludes any representation, any "idea" of the limit.


◆　*"Do we really want to occupy ourselves with them?"*—*"They have already fallen into our worklessness."*—*"We watch over them."*—*"But it is they who keep watch."*—*"We observe them, we guard them."*


◆　The idea of the threshold, in as much as it is a regula-tory idea, and in the way of a concept, is all the same general, while the "threshold" does not allow us to designate by the same word "ethical threshold", "political threshold", "artistic threshold", without reintroducing the threshold into the common space and dissolving it there.

◆    *"They do not love us, knowing nothing about us."*— *"That is their way of loving us, they are at our side."*

◆    *They did not say: "I am afraid", but: "fear". And at once fear filled the universe.*

◆    *"We live for those who know nothing about us."*—*"Ah, they also live for us, and even more so since they don't know it."*—*"But what do they have to do with our life?"*
    *There was something disturbing about feeling them thus exposed and as if given up by the care which we supposed they took to avoid us.*
    *Impenetrable, as if they concealed themselves by their transparency.*

◆    Everything must efface itself, everything will efface itself. This is in accordance with the infinite demand of effacement that writing take place and take its place.
    Even if writing leaves traces, and, leaving them, makes traces engender themselves and produce themselves out of the life of traces? One can answer: to write is to go by way of the world of traces, towards the effacement of traces and of all traces, since traces are opposed to totality and always already disperse themselves. Another response: writing marks, but does not leave marks. More precisely: there is between mark and traces such a difference that it almost accounts for the equivocal nature of writing. Writing marks and leaves traces, but the traces do not depend on the mark and, at the limit, are

not in relation to it. The traces do not refer to the moment of the mark, they are without origin, but not without end in the very permanence that seems to perpetuate them, traces which, even in becoming confused and replacing each other, are there forever, and forever cut off from that of which they would be the traces, having no other being than their plurality, as if there were not *a* trace, but traces, never the same and always repeated. The *mark* of writing. To mark is in a certain way not to leave marks and only, by this active lack of marks, failure to distribute plurally in a well delimited space, already to demand the line of *demarcation* not to cross and yet to demand it as from its crossing in view of a completely *other* space. To mark is, by this separation of mark and traces, to make the traces not refer to the mark as to their beginning and always multiply and superimpose themselves, traces by traces, not to be deciphered, but to efface themselves plurally.

The mark, it is to be absent from the present and to make the present be absent. And the trace, being always traces, does not refer to any initial presence that would still be present, as remainder or vestige, there where it has disappeared.


◆     *As attentive as they can be—and to such a degree that we do not know it—they ask more attention of us than we will ever grant them.*


◆     A brusque and fortuitous speech, unjust and refined (always taken out of the exchange): sinister possibility that is like the gift of innocent language.


◆     *"Ah, we no longer speak like we used to speak."—"You find me worse?"—"Very bad."—"Well, I won't change any more: there's only one possible change left."—"We've been dying for so long and for so little time."*

♦ The time when all these truths are stories, when all stories are false: no present, nothing but what is actual.


♦ To write: work of the absence of work, production that produces nothing except (or out of) the absence of a subject, mark that unmarks, infinitive in which the infinite would like to play itself out even to the neuter: to write does not depend on the present and does not make it raise itself. And yet to write, if it is not declined, if it also rejects, and with even less ambiguity, the past mode and the future mode so that have written or will write can only *be written,* tends, in order to lighten itself, to maintain itself in a conditional without condition (would write, would have written), letting itself thus be projected into the sky of the ideal, where the unreal would realize itself dangerously and illusorily. That is dangerous indeed: writing could not write itself in the conditional (Mallarmé and all of us with him, have we not felt this attraction? "Who knows what would be needed for that?"); the modesty of the conditional is misleading in seeming to put into question only personal failure or to attest to writing's position of impossibility (which would be impossible, not as the "real" is, but as the pure Good would be, except in heaven), while writing takes place, whether this be never, rarely, at every instant in the absence of time, but precisely as place that precedes every "taking place", mark of which we know only the traces because of which we give it as lost, effaced, or as unrepresentable effacement. When these formulations with which we play: to write is not to have written, but would be, in the suddeness that leaves no trace, to have always already written as that which will always write itself anew. Formulation not without authority, since, through it, we seem to shatter the articulated modes of the present, future, past, but through their use itself. From this, once again, to write as response to the affirmation of the return and, immediately, as that to which the return, which could affirm itself only in the form of writing, responds.

♦     "To write.—Later.—Later: slowly, according to the plain gentleness of the interrupted that never relates itself to a future of time, no more than it poses itself in the present moment."


♦     The "not yet" of thought, this failure of the present in regard to what there would be to think, always implied in every presence of thought, the ambiguity of such a "not yet" could not distribute its resources, once it is a matter of writing.
Writing carries away, tears away, through the plural dispersion of its practice, every horizon as well as every foundation, carrying away through a carrying away that does not have time to unfold itself, which one could thus say was sudden, like a mark that would not have time (having all time) to leave traces, taking away the limit that is only such under the demand of an "always already", forbidden through its transgression or uncrossable if or as soon as already crossed, and immediately and at the same time diverted from every crossing (from every openness)[6]. The "not yet" of thought, the "always already" of writing inscribe themselves according to the intervals that each maintain or sets free, but that do not superimpose themselves on one another.


♦     It would seem that writing has life as its support, even though thought would hold on to time as the process of its accomplishment.


♦     The essential power to neglect the fact that writing would have life for support, finds itself facilitated and theoretically justified by the resource of books. Books seem to be there to preserve writing and to allow it to constitute itself in its own space, separate and as if separated from any life. Writing, forced to give itself as the expression or affirmation of

56

life, has never satisfied either writing or life. The refined categories, those of existence, the play of being and of time, offered to the question of writing, have been able to serve to keep such a question "alive", but without giving us any illusion about this "borrowed" life. Life contests writing that conceals itself from life or reduces it. But the contest comes from writing that leaves plenitude to life and unexceptionable presence to the Living, bearer of life, while writing can certainly propose itself as that which would exhaust life in order to inscribe itself at the limit of life; finally the proposition makes room for this other, completely other: writing only writes itself at the limit of writing, there where the book, although still there, is the pressure of the end (without end) of books.

◆ To write at the limit of writing: but everything is played out in the difference of these repeated terms. Difference held by the very repetition whose possibility escapes, being given over to the difference that has necessarily always already repeated itself, even though it will always repeat itself, without being able to be spoken in such a way that it repeats itself in the present.

◆ *When he crossed it, the city murmured in him constantly: I am afraid, be the witness of fear.*

◆ *He carries fear, fear does not belong to him: intransportable fear, without anyone to feel it, destitute of all, fear, the lack of fear.*

◆ *Fear for the one who is afraid, who does not know it: the collapsed center of empty fear.*
*Fear, that which does not have death as a limit, even the infinite death of others; nevertheless, I am afraid for the others*

*who are afraid of dying, who will die without me, in the distancing of this self which would vainly replace theirs.*

♦   *Let fear leave me to interrogate fear: "But why are you afraid?"—"Don't ask me: I'm afraid."—"Are you afraid, in this way, even to the point of fear?"—"You ask me this, you shouldn't have asked me this."—"But I ask it in the same way that you're afraid: my question is your fear."*

♦   Fear, we call it mortal, while it hides the death towards which it attracts us from us; but fear, always exceding the self in which it entrenches itself, absent from the one who carries it, as from the language that pronounces it, making us strangers to ourselves, is the fear for *someone* who does not let himself be approached and whom death already turns away from our rescue, although it is called for, awaited.

♦   *"Someone who is afraid does not know it, does not call for help."—"But it is for him that I'm afraid, one time and always from then on."*

♦   We say pain, we say unhappiness. But fear?

♦   *Fear, as if he recalled this word that made him forget everything.*

♦   *Fear, it is this gift that they would give us in the posthumous city; the possibility of being afraid for them: fear given in the word fear; fear not felt.*

♦     *Neither of them was given to using tricks: he, being a part of his plans that supposed a life that was still intact, the everyday life promised to all, and he, hearing nothing but the speech that was already failing, incapable of speaking except by default. Between them, the responsibility of fear.*

♦     *"It's true, I am afraid."—"You say this so calmly."—"Saying it, however, does not alleviate the fear: on the contrary, it the word fear that henceforth makes me afraid; having said it no longer allows me to say anything else."—"But, 'I am afraid', I also: because of this word, spoken so calmly: as no one, as if no one were afraid."—"From now on, it is the whole language that is afraid."*

♦     This fear of language, it was incumbent on him not to see in it anything but the possibility, always open, that any word, belonging to the order of words that are only such by their belonging to language, could turn on this language in order to detach itself from it and to raise itself above it in mastering it, perhaps in shattering it, at least in pretending to assign it a limit. Fear does not signify that language would be afraid, even metaphysically, but that fear is a piece of language, something that it would have lost and that would make it entirely dependent on this dead piece: entirely, that is, precisely in reconstituting itself without unity, piece by piece, as something other than a collection of significations. Certainly, metaphor intervenes finally to hold in suspense, making it inoffensive, the possibility of language's being other than a process of meaning. Through metaphor, the fear of language becomes the fear of speaking or the fear which, being the essence of any speech, would make any use of speech, as any silence, frightening. The fear of language: the fear that strikes language when it loses a word that is then *a surplus word, a word too many:* fear, God, madness. Or the "he/it" displaced from its rank and role of subject.

◆    Why these names so heavy, too charged with themselves, as charged with all the surcharge of language, over
which they are called to stand? God is thus a name, pure
materiality, naming nothing, not even himself. Whence the
perversion, magical, mystical, literal, of the name, the opacity
of God to any idea of God. And still, like fear, like madness, it
disappears, if only as a messenger of another language, of
which such a disappearance could not take the place of a
beginning. The "death of God" is perhaps only the help that
historical language vainly brings to allow a word to fall outside of language without another announcing itself there: absolute slip.


◆    *And we do nothing but repeat. Nocturnal repetition, rep-*
*etition of the one who says: is it this, to die, is it this, fear?*


◆    He who, in the street, stops the unknown woman with
the dark eyes and says to her: *"I am afraid, don't you want to*
*accompany me for a moment?"*, gives her the movement of fear
as a companion forever. But he entrusts his thought to her,
the safeguard of this endangered thought, replacing itself in
the unknown—the unknown that nevertheless has a face, the
face of the unknown—by a call that escapes not only the pro-
priety of relations, but the human relation of relations, and
thus is a mark of what one must call unreasonableness. One
must, then, go by way of madness, here maintained within the
limits of an initiative that is only hazardous, to take a step
outside of madness, in the slip that brushes the outside. There
is certainly something unreasonable in forgetting—in not
being aware—that every human being is not immediately the
*other* whose thought—that is, whose madness—could be par-
doned each time, by a word (barely a word, a murmur difficult
to hear). And since the unknown one welcomes in such a simple way, taking gently by the hand he who has stopped her
and helping him cross the night, as one helps a blind person
cross the street, that one can conclude nothing from such a

60

movement of welcoming, from this improbable possibility open between beings, open through that which could not be shared (the separation of "madness"), this is what makes reason vacillate anew, even in giving it to keep, on condition that one does not conclude anything from it (does not make sense of it) this disturbance that does not belong to it.

Any conclusion, any interpretation, would be a delirious one, a temptation of thought to reestablish a relation of equilibrium between itself and its Other. To say: that is a sign of Goodness, somebody does Good for me, is to deprive this human girl, who would probably have refused to be called good or to have done anything good, of herself, as she is well on this side of and well beyond any goodness. To say: that would be so in a perfect society, everyone welcoming everyone else without asking for anything, is to forget that madness or fear would be in some way forbidden in this society or restored to the community itself, in order that it take care of them, without any particular person being able, except by mistake, to accept this sick particularity and to allow it a refuge. To say: he who entrusts himself absolutely finds already in the limitlessness of trust a response to the enclosed speech, having carried his fear as far as friendship—fraternity without law—, is to make a law of that which, having taken place only once and still, from that, taking place all the time, announces itself as impossible, real in as much as impossible. He who has received this sign knows immediately that not only is there no right, but that all those who, far from being welcomed as he was, have been rejected, drag this after them from then on with no recourse but the great river. How then pretend to acquit oneself of the "event" in speaking of luck or of chance, word at once reduced to its poverty, especially when the other is *in play* in it.

♦     *Is it this, to die, is it this, fear?* The silent dread, and this silence, like a cry without words; mute, although crying endlessly.

♦     *Dread: "Do nothing, and it is still too much."—"Then let me cease to be."—"Do not tamper with your being."*

*What is left for you to do: to undo yourself in this nothing that you do.*


♦     If I am in dread as in truth, it is a truth that already deceives me and that I, meanwhile, can leave behind only in deceiving myself.

Once we have passed a certain threshold, never knowing we have done so although knowing it, in an uncertainty which is already its mark, everything belongs to dread, including non-dread, it is a trap, and still it is without ruse, there is a loyalty, a simplicity, a tranquility of dread, perhaps because it escapes every law; wildness with the calm of the forests, the calm of a wait for something that will not take place.


♦     *A double meaning: the noise of the city with its interpretable richness, always ready to be named, then the same noise like the sound of the waves, monotonous, wild, inaudible, with sudden and unforeseeable bursts being a part of the monotony.*


♦     There is an "I don't know" that is at the limit of knowledge, but that belongs to knowledge. Always, we pronounce it too early, still knowing everything—or too late, when I no longer know that I don't know, saying nothing and thus saying it.

I know less about it than I know about it; it is over this being behind itself of knowledge that I must leap to reach—not attaining it, or ruining myself in it—unknowledge.


♦     Dread—horror of all that names it, and, naming it, identifies it, glorifies it. It wants this: that one not speak of it,

62

and that, since as soon as one speaks it is it that speaks, one says nothing.

Dread of letting dread speak or, silencing it, letting it occupy all of the silence.

Dread—this word that cannot be pronounced, that one would like to silence in crying out, with its inappropriateness, its philosophic and pathetic pretension; but, turned away from me, "I" receive it from others as the unknown of all pain, the supplication of a powerless care.

♦ Dread makes reading forbidden (the words separated, something arid and devastating about them; no more texts, every word useless, or else foundering in something that I do not know, attracting me to it with resistance, understanding as an injustice). To write, then, effect of a negative hallucination, giving nothing to read, nothing to understand.

♦ When dread forbids dread, preventing my being abandoned to it in order to better hold on to me. "You will not transgress me."—"I will not sanctify you." The unsureness of certain dread.

♦ *It is like a figure that he doesn't see, that is missing because it is there, having all the traits of a figure that would not figure itself and with which the incessant lack of relation, without presence, without absence, is a sign of a common solitude. He names it, although he knows that it has no name, even in his language, this beating of a hesitant heart. Neither of them lives, life passes between them, leaving them on the edge of space.*

*Wordless in the midst of words.*

♦ The favorable fragment.

◆ He could no longer ask; dread is also this detour of the question, the obstacle to its being a question about dread. The unknown of dread interrogates us, but does not let itself be interrogated: the failure before that which does not let itself be interrogated.

◆ *Would they live without the strength and energy that the desire to die gives them?*

◆ Dread does not keep busy, preventing one from doing anything, preventing the very enjoyment or complaint of boredom.

◆ He is not skeptical enough to hope. He does not hope enough to stop at nihilism. The unknown without hope. Dread: the unsureness that excludes the uncertainty of doubt, what decisiveness is left for doubt to exert itself.

Inattentive as if in the power of a constant attention. A thought that he does not identify, even knowing it, holds vigil. One would say that it is there to prohibit mortal surprise, being this surprise itself.

◆ *The desire to die growing weary, there remained for them nothing but to die.*

*Not entreating the stars for anything, to die thoughtlessly. To desire, to cease to have any relation to the gaze, to turn oneself away from heaven; desire is this detour by which "I" stop thinking about myself; it thus has a relation to the night without stars, this night of slowness, of insufficiency: drifting without shore.*

◆ *At night, towards the night. Future dream, sleep undone. To die of night.*

*It is in the morning, in the brief mist that eternalizes itself, that he expires of night.*

♦   *He no longer delimits himself, he fragments himself.*

♦   The temptation: the fragment favorable, as if, in its non-unity, this could be alone, the last, the last, without brevity, without place, obstinacy in reverse, its speech of the infinite at last dissuaded, taken back into its gentleness.

♦   A word chosen by the dread foreign to any choice in its immense oscillating work, the work of dread, its hammer of ruin, dread seeking refuge in dread.

The distant always near to dread, its trace effaced, retraced: never whole, morcellated, hammered, with something young about it that is frightening.

♦   Sparse brevity, perservering, become slowness that interrupts itself, like a suffering has always returned and that does not recognize me. Its arrogance is my supplication.

The smallness of dread, my whole always surpassed—that which keeps me from being whole with myself, with you. The incessant intermittence.

♦   *Silence, I know you by hearsay.*

♦   *He is in a closed world whose closing is the only event that produces itself in it.*

♦   *What decision had he made that put him out of reach, although friendly, close?*

◆     Between the silence and the silence, exchanged word—innocent murmur.


◆     Sedentary dread.


◆     Turned away from the unique, under the fascination of the multiple, he does not carry several ideas or an infinity of contradictory ideas: the multiple rarefies, singularizes.


◆     *In me there is someone who does nothing but undo this me: infinite occupation.*


◆     To the one who has asked so many questions, death comes softly as the lost question.


◆     To die would be, every time there where we speak, that which holds back from affirming, from affirming itself, as from denying. That is heard, understood: we believe we hear it, but it is tacit; even the rustling of dread stops.


◆     At the limit, to die; but it is life without dread.


◆     Alone again, offered to the multiple, in the plurality of dread, outside himself, signaling without calling, one dissuaded by the other. Solitude is evidently space without place, when presence calls itself non-presence, where nothing is one—challenge, without distrust, to the unique. Solitude hides me from solitude, sometimes.

66

Alone again, challenge to the unique, one lost for the other.

♦ The trait of dread: it repels any why, it does not respond to a lack; the absence of a why of dread does not, however, lead to restfulness, nor to any glory, but to a risk so great that dying no longer seems an outlet to escape from it; what risk? the risk of the unknown without question, without risk.

♦ Supposing that dread is innocence itself, an innocence apparently unknown, man feels guilty for not being able to bear innocence, guilty of this innocence that anguishes him.

♦ Dying "frees" us from dread (dying, this re-emanating of impossible death, the distant proximity) as dread is unaware of dying; both, however, faultless: the unknown that differs.

♦ Unknowledge would like to pass itself off as a response to dread's absence of why. But it is its empty echo, its immobile repetition, unless, repeating it or preceding it, it is this night in which dread has already lost itself under the attraction of the loss that it maintains and that maintains it, night without speech of the night without image.

♦ The sad mouth spoke peacefully.

♦ "Enter into the destructive element," we do not write a word that does not contain this invitation and, sometimes, another that is superfluous: let you destroy yourself.

There are no words in the language of dread to say: that is possible.

♦ Defiance or derision: *he listens to the silence with words.*

♦ What can be repeated is only what could not be, the unreplaced, the singular in which the One has disappeared in its simulacrum. As if there were repetition only there where there would be absence of law. Repetition of the extreme: general collapse; the neuter, that which expires without producing itself.

♦ Dread without suspicion, openess of the detour, unburdened of fear, raising itself above protests, accepting every refusal: thought; loss of thought.

Dread, if it desubjugates the subject, not authorizing it, refusing it authority (experience), is dread through and through in that it is not felt.

♦ I do not know; there is no "I" to not know.

♦ Loss is impossible.—It passes through the impossible.—It is in this that it is really loss, loss of thought, never compensated.—Loss is demand, it demands of thought that it be un-thought[7], loss of loss (without annulment of return): only repeating, falling due (luck that does not fall due) of the neuter.

The leap of questioning would have the neuter as its support, leaping over itself, in an immobile fall.

68

◆ But we can always ask ourselves about the neuter, interrogating it through the dread that turns the question away, repeating it, throwing it back into silence, the silence which does not silence itself.

◆ enter/between: enter/between/neuter/not being[8]. Play, play without the happiness of playing, with the residue of a letter that would call to the night by the lure of a negative presence. The night radiates the night to the very neuter in which it extinguishes itself.

◆ The enigma of the neuter, enigma that the neuter reduces even in making it shine in a name.

◆ *"Is it you?"—"Yes, it's me."—"You, in broad daylight."— "In the broad daylight of darkness."*
*When he came to his house, in broad daylight, exchanging the greeting for darkness.*

◆ *Crossing the distances, alone to hear, not to hear, giving the voice a voice, voice of no one once again. "Listen."— "Listen." In the silence something was speaking, something was being quiet. Truth gives no news.*

◆ *To cross the distant, to turn the distant back toward the distant without approach.*

◆ The distant calls to the near, repelling it, not to define itself in it by opposition, nor to form a couple with it by resemblance and difference, but in such a way that the separation between the two still belongs to the distant. The near, repelling it, calls to the immediate that consumes it. The near is always only near. The proximity of presence does not make itself present, because presence is never near, it has always already affirmed the absolute of presence which is there one time and for all without relation nor progression, nor dawn nor dusk. The near, through presence, belongs to the distant, and through the distant, belongs to the indefinite play of separation and limit. Indecision is what brings together near and far: both unsituated, unsituable, never given in a place or a time, but each its own variation of time and place. Where the distant, where the near? To distance oneself, to approach: let us admit that the verb has significance before the noun; distancing oneself supposes a fixed point in relation to which there would be distancing; this fixed point is once again presence; distancing does not stop distancing itself, because there is no term to distancing, even though there is no beginning to the distant. One can certainly say: he distances himself, but he is still near, one can say this, even though one has the feeling that the infinite power of distancing gets in the way of any determination of the "near", which has as a point of reference not the distant, but rather the vicinity of presence that excludes any neighboring. The near is thus repelled by the absolute of presence and held apart, taken back into the separation of the distant: unable thus to mediate the two terms or even to "bring them closer together", still less able to maintain them together in a necessity of thought. The near would not bring near, it lacks the being of presence, lack that is its mark and that is not only a lack of presence, but the lack that the multiple distant carries.


◆    Approaching is distancing's game. The game of distant and near is the game of the distant. Approaching the distances is the formula that tries to make the distances burst in contact with a presence thus characterized by distance, as in a certain way it always is; thus again presence and distance are linked; distant presence, distant of presence, the distances would be present there. The near alone, then, would be safe from contamination by a presence. To be near is to not be present. The near promises that it will never take hold. Praise for the approach of that which escapes: the next death, the distance of the next death.

♦   To distance oneself: he distances himself, but I never distance myself. "I" entails being there, decisive presence that does not let itself be affected by any distancing. Whoever says "I" still says presence. Divine ubiquity is this power of presence which has always already annexed itself to being-present; certainly god is the distant *par excellence,* but the distant that has presence for its truth, a distance of pure presence. The distant and the near are dimensions of what escapes presence as well as absence under the attraction of the "he/it". He/it distances him-/it-self, he/it approaches, the same spectered affirmation, the same premises of non-presence.

♦   There would be a separation of time, like a separation of place, belonging neither to time nor to place. In this separation, we would come to the point of writing.

♦   *"I would like to attract them in their name."—"An excellent name, certainly."—"A name forgotten, no longer in use."—"We forget nothing."—"When they take on this name that is under any name, they will walk with a sure step, crossing the distances, towards us."*

♦   *The lips suspended from the night, they did not speak the night.*

♦     Proximity once again says something against presence
(dissuades presence): what is near is too near for it to be only
presence; through proximity, I can say "you" [*toi*] (even if this
is in the night of words), thus can pronounce an intimacy that
makes presence burst to pieces, abolishing it in some way or
making it great to the point that it is destroyed. So I can say:
"You are so near that you are not present", but near to whom?
precisely near to whom and not to me: thus, I know that, in
the figure of a "you" falsely called forth, what is said is once
more: he is so near that he is there outside among the signs
borne by the distant.


♦     *He lived there, the house reconstructed itself around
him, I saw him behind the window, waiting without hearing
me, exhausting the overfullness of our words through the wait.*


♦     *He concluded from this, in the course of his always more
rare comings and goings, that they would never be there, even
in passing, but soberly, austerely, there below, prescribed (pro-
scribed) by their name: near or far, with the approval of that
which gives no approval—chance.*


♦     We can always ask ourselves about the neuter. The neuter is first of all attested to by certain grammars. The Greek *to*
is perhaps the first occurence in our tradition, surprising for
its lack of clamor, which marks with a sign—it is true, among
others—the decision of a new language, a language later
taken over by philosophy at the price of this neuter that introduces it. The neuter in the singular names something that
escapes nomination, but without making any noise, without
even the noisiness of an enigma. We call it, modestly, thoughtlessly, the thing. The thing: because, from all the evidence,
things belong to another order and things are what are most
familiar, without being transparent, making us live in our

environment of things. Things are illuminated, but do not let light pass through them, even if they are themselves made of grains of light, thus reducing the light to opacity. The thing, like the he/it, like the neuter or the outside, indicates a plurality characterized by singularizing itself and by appearing, by default, to rest in the indeterminate. That the Thing has a relation to the Neuter: outrageous and finally inadmissible supposition, insofar as the neuter cannot arrest itself in a subject noun, even if this be collective, having also this movement of diverting anything to which it would apply itself from its momentaneous essence, its meaning and its definition. "The thing is in relation to the Neuter" forces us immediately to think that the neuter changes the relation into non-relation, and the Thing into another thing, and the neuter into what could not be the Neuter itself, nor that which neutralizes. Perhaps—a perhaps that would also mean certainly—we are wrong, naming the neuter, to name it, as if it were not "itself" in the neuter, forgetting, besides, that even in being a grammatical category, thus belonging primarily to language, it is borne by the whole language, as if language "in general" were neuter, since, on the basis of the neuter, all the forms and possibilities of affirmation and negation unfold themselves in it. The neuter is thus implicated in the functioning of every language, even in occupying its silent other side and preventing it from being reduced to a complex game of interminable structures, or to the sedimentary presence of some living speech. The neuter, authorized by grammar, in complicity with all languages and, in language, with the part of it that is neither active nor passive, neither transitive nor intransitive, indicating in the form of a noun, a verbal way of holding back the demand to speak, continues to swarm in a mythology in which, if it is in play, it is never definitively committed. The neuter: we think we grasp it if we invoke forms of passive action as marked and remarkable as those, precisely, of chance, of the random, of the unconscious, of the trace and of the game. And many other forms could be proposed without ever satisfying: the *sacred* in relation to *god;* absence in relation to *presence, writing* (taken here as non-exemplary example) in relation to *speech,* the *other* in relation to *me* (and to this me that the other is as well), *being* in relation to *existence, difference* in relation to the *one.* The neuter, without letting itself be known (though it were at the price of an absolute knowledge), recognizes itself, or rather, plays, in each of these terms characterized by their not being easily conceptualizable, and, perhaps, not being so because with them is introduced a negative possibility of a type so particular that one could neither mark it with a negation nor affirm it. The Neuter, by a simple literal affinity, inclines toward the Night, although there is no closeness between them semantically. The Neuter does not have the ancient mythological names that any night carries with it. The Neuter derives, in the most simple way, from a negation of two terms: *neuter,* neither one nor the other. Neither nor the other, nothing more precise. What remains is that affirmation already has, in advance, and before any denegation, its part in the neuter: the one the other—*qu/uter,* which of the two?—signifies also one of the two and in some way that which is never only one. "One and the other" seems, by this bipartition—unequal and at the same time badly determined, although of very ancient usage—to allude to the archaic necessity of an apparently binary reading (as if everything had to begin by two), but of a binarity that at once loses its dual value and pluralizes itself to the point of indeterminacy: one, yes, this can be indicated with the finger; but other is the other, entirely other and always other; it flees itself in fleeing us. Obviously, the expression, "one and the other", even in indicating a division that is meant to clarify (one/all the rest, but at the same time only the other, including the other of all the rest), thus indicating a reading that reads by going back and forth constantly, from one term to a second term, is marked, "altered" by the perverse predominance of the *other,* which is not to say by a play of words. The neuter perhaps does nothing but take in this perversity of the other in making it still more perverse by the obscurity that covers it without dissipating it, without attaining a true negation (nor ever, redoubled and not reversed, a negation of negation) capable of repose or clarity. The neuter takes the other back into itself under a light (but impenetrable) veil that seems only to force out of the other its

74

incessant affirmation that a negative alone allows us to grasp: the other of the other, the un-known of the other, its refusal to let itself be thought as the other than the one, and its refusal to be only the Other or the "other than". The neuter puts all that to rest, even in silently withdrawing repose. The neuter, by its nominal, thus positive, form, allows to be juxtaposed—makes play themselves out—an affirmation and an indefinite series of negation: it does not put them together for a dialectical reversal; this is in fact one of the peculiarities of its contribution, the affirmation by which what is in play would be neither one nor the other—affirmation that endlessly makes an echo of itself to the point of dispersion, dispersion going even to the very silence dispersed,—is not really affirmative or operative; its work, which consisted of veiling the other in showing it off under the veil and also in putting a stop to the bad infinite (at work in the other), in putting it back into play though a negative scansion, is only pseudo-work. Something is at work by way of the neuter that is immediately the work of worklessness: there is an effect of the neuter—this says something of the passivity of the neuter—that is not an effect *of the* neuter, not being the effect of a Neuter pretendedly at work as a cause or a thing. There would then not be a work of the neuter as one speaks of a work of the negative. The Neuter: paradoxical name: it barely speaks, mute word, simple, yet always veiling itself, always displacing itself out of its meaning, operating invisibly on itself while not ceasing to unwind itself, in the immobility of its position that repudiates depth. It neutralizes, neutralizes (itself), thus evokes (does nothing but evoke) the movement of *Aufhebung,* but if it suspends and retains, it retains only the movement of suspending, that is, the distance it creates by the fact that, occupying the terrain, it makes the distance disappear. The Neuter, then, designates difference in indifference, opacity in transparency, the negative scansion of the other, which can reproduce itself only by the averted attraction—omitted—of the one. Even the negation of the Neuter is concealed. The neuter that would mark "being" does not thus refer it back to the crudeness of non-being, but has always already dispersed being itself as that which, giving itself neither as this nor as that, also refuses to present itself in simple presence, letting itself be grasped only negatively, under the protective veil of the no. If being reads itself, writes itself in the neuter, it is not, however, the case that the neuter comes before being, nor only that the neuter would give itself under the veil of the difference between being and beings, neither being nor beings (rather the beyond of the two or the hither of the between-the-two), but that the neuter averts it in gently dissuading it from any presence, even a negative one, neutralizing it to the point of preventing it from being called the being of the neuter, even while leading it into the infinite erosion of negative repetition.

The Neuter marks being, effect of every mark: the being marked in the neuter is not remarked and always forgets, in the brilliance of being, this mark of which even the brilliance is only an effect.

The Neuter does not come first, eternal follower that precedes, so that the neuter is nowhere, functioning in language in every place as play of the mark, if that which marks unmarks, and, in the end, neutralizes as far as the line of demarcation that there could be no question, crossing it, of crossing. The transgression that is accomplished as not being accomplished, if it is also affirmed in the neuter, in the neutrality of a never present lure, could not, at least not as a proposition, mark the neuter as that which, always at play in transgression, would be precisely that which was to be transgressed. As if writing, the incessant movement of writing, freed us from the game of writing.

◆     The Neuter, the gentle prohibition against dying, there where, from threshold to threshold, eye without gaze, silence carries us into the proximity of the distant. Word still to be spoken beyond the living and the dead, *testifying to the absence of testimony.*

◆     *"We are there together as forgetfulness and memory; you remember, I forget; I remember, you forget." He stopped for a*

76

*moment: "It's as if they were there at the threshold, going from threshold to threshold. One day they will enter, they will know that we know." The time comes when the time will come.*

*"We know only their name."—". . . in which they do enter but by which they attract us."*


◆    The Neuter, would it be neuter, would it be that which conceals itself in concealing and concealing even the act of concealing, with nothing of what disappears in this way appearing, an effect reduced to the absence of effect: the neuter, in the articulation of the visible-invisible, inequality, still, of the equal, a response to the impatient question (that which classes and determines in advance by dividing in two, without precaution: which of the two?), but a response that, immediately and unnoticably, although appearing to welcome the question, modifies its structure by its refusal not only to choose, but to submit itself to the possibility of a choice between two terms: such as one or the other, yes or no, this or that, day night, god or man. "Which of the two?"—"Neither one nor the other, the other, the other", as if the neuter spoke only in an echo, meanwhile perpetuating the other by the repetition that difference, always included in the other, even in the form of the bad infinite, calls forth endlessly: the balancing of a man's head given over to eternal oscillation.


◆    The improper of the neuter is, perhaps, in the continuity of meaning that any name proposes, while this word does not stop echoing within itself in order to withdraw itself from the continuity. The neuter is improper, but even that is not its property.

The neuter wears down the sharp edge of the negative, wears out the dull affirmation of the neuter; would the neuter in its disinterestedness be the mark of the desire understood as the error of that which, always in advance, in its omitted attraction, has separated itself from any desire?

◆     *Since their coming, meanwhile, the essential had been
the astonishing character of everything, because if he had
thought, generously and lucidly, that he was capable of regis-
tering a shock that would have found him ready to let himself
be moved from top to bottom, he realized that, failing presence,
and with the exception of a change in the way in which they
had to get used to speaking to one another from now on, he
could not decide what would make him capable of letting himself be astonished among all the unmodified things. It is true
that this friend had disappeared. Since when, he could not
say; they had for so long been used to speaking to each other
from afar, from near, through the rumors of the city, or even
through the repetition of an ancient language, always ready to
give them a place in its game. The fact that they saw each other
was, they realized, only a derivative mode of their right to
speak to one another, right that it was up to him not to let
prescribe. They spoke to each other, they saw each other, there
was in this a sort of good use of their constant cordiality, itself
an expression, but to a much higher degree, of the relations
each could not help having with all. Still, did he not have to
recognize the exceptional character of relations that were not at
all friendly, nor only trusting, that were, on the contrary, difficult, forbidden each time and almost private, even if it were
convenient for him to make them count as personal conversa-
tions, known and recognized in advance as such among so
many others? Exceptional, this word resonated like a low-
pitched sound in several registers at once, always below the
lowest vibrations, those which he still liked to muffle. Exceptional, he remembered the complacency with which, not without a certain derision always implied in their seriousness, they
agreed to act as if these relations could be deserving of this
title, if only to make them more acceptable. That was not delib-
erate, at least on his part—but what was his part, what did he
get outside of his role, which was, moreover, interchangeable,
in exchanges that were never imposed on him except in his
being haunted by memories over which he had so little control
that he began to believe that they did not belong to him, memory of nobody, rather? He remembered, no doubt, memory so
ancient of a Thing that could not be called present, nor to*

78

*come, only less ancient than the memory which he felt strike him—strike him gently, almost affectionately, in the way that at night, in the night, timid words crossed his sleep: sudden, nevertheless. It was, further, of sleep that he must have thought when, paying him the usual visit, he must have noticed the room that was suddenly immense, surrounded by books, as if to accentuate the emptiness of the space, where it seemed that the whole town, if it had wanted to, could have spread itself out, with the great central river and its immobile borderers, derangement of perspective that was corrected by the slightness of the person, seated very far away in a corner on a chair, very old—like a reminiscence rather than a memory— shrunken, as someone who had waited too long might have shrunk, without one's knowing to what wait he still hoped to respond. This had reawakened his ancient fear, a fear repressed by the memory of his fear, and while he prepared to cross, as he had crossed the outlying areas of the town, the great bare rooms where—in what place?—it would have been granted him to meet his friend, he came up against the words: "I was not sure of the time of our meeting", by which the rules, or, as he would have said, the necessary conventions, were affirmed once more. "Yes, I'm late."—"Late, you are always perfectly punctual."—"Still, lagging behind my memory: as if it happened that, following the eternal straight road, I found myself alone and suddenly, as, however, I had always feared would happen, tested by the risky words that we had intentionally pronounced about* them: *dangerous words,* words of the blind."—*"Words of the blind, indeed; these are what are needed; but haven't we agreed to take on the risk together?"— "Yes, together, but the risk also threatens us in this."—"Has it occurred to you that the risk could begin by refusing to leave us together to speak?"—"The risk that such words, such voices without regard, propose to us, is too great for us to have been able to formulate it with the same words."—"But whatever had happened, it would have been necessary, since it had already been said, that you come around to saying it."—"To saying it again, but not necessarily to saying it and even less to saying it to you."—"To me, of course, before you." And while he listened as if there had been something there not to hear, he added:*

*"Say it, be brave, let the words go. Tell me what happened."*—
*"It's that you had disappeared." To his surprise, he did not take
this lightly: he remained silent, pushing this answer, already
completely prepared, away, and only saying, a little later, with
some agitation: they arrive, they arrive. It is from this that he
got the feeling he should no longer leave him.*


♦    the straight roads, eternal, under a scratched out sky


♦    *"But what shadow of presence would I have if I had not
at each moment already disappeared?"* What a strange emptiness is the lack of an answer.


♦    *They remembered, but what they remembered was always less ancient than their memory.*


♦    *"I know."—"I know."—"We don't know."*


♦    Page unfolded by the void of writing


♦    Later on he maintained—although it was perhaps an
indiscreet way of maintaining himself among the words in
front of a friend—this affirmation that, at present, called
forth by an exhortation to courage, did not simply constitute a
new possibility of relations with this friend, but opened the
way to something that it was not possible for him to establish
alone. He had bravely confirmed that he would not abandon
him, but *that their good alliance, not being a lasting or regular
pact, did not put a privilege to which they could refer at any*

*moment into their hands. To which he answered that perhaps*
*the ruse that had allowed them to say that they were close had*
*slipped into their game of words, words less conventional, ca-*
*pable of making any attempt to discourage them fail. "I know*
*what you think: you hold me solidly in your memory."—"On*
*condition that you remember me." While he watched him, now*
*that he was at the end of his voyage, unable, although he was*
*certainly very near him, to help confusing him with the*
*shrunken person whom he saw in the distance of the straight*
*road, like a figure that space, after having played with it a lot,*
*would have had to abandon on the shore, he affirmed his*
*agreement anew; they are coming, not without adding: the*
*Thing remembers us.*

♦      *When he crossed it, the city, as if it had been deserted*
*and without distance.*

♦      Distancing oneself appears to be determined in relation
to a fixed point that would be presence. But presence, in the
absolute of the immediate in which, great instantaneous fire,
it consumes itself endlessly, could not be fixed or included in
the game of a relation. Presence, lightning of presence, which
has always already devastated the space in which the approach takes place, does not enter into the clarity of the visible, no more than it lets itself be present. Presence lacks
presence, destroys the present of presence.

♦      *The only way, it seemed to him, not to make too tangible,*
*without, however, effacing its effect, the affirmation that he*
*had brought him, an affirmation like the junction of all kinds*
*of decisions having different meanings, which did not grant*
*him any respite, was to let it do its work in taking it up again*
*endlessly into their language and as a simple moment of this*
*language. For, even if he still felt apprehensive to speak about*

81

*it, since apprehension was accessory to it, he felt above all surprise, to hear the word claim some kind of brilliance: that this friend had disappeared, carried, carried off, by the great wave of his perpetual memory, did not prevent him, with his usual benevolence, from answering for the disappearance himself, both as if nothing had happened and as if he had had to draw out, in his presence, all the consequences of his unfortunate admission. The consequence developed slowly, but also immediately, with the suddenness of an unforeseeable resolution. While it seemed to him that he would from now on have to make an effort to join him, as the other was maintaining himself in a fiction of distancing even when he was present, it would be his person that bore the intensity, be it as a being unalterably shrunken, he saw him behind his table, seated comfortably and sumptuously, majestic character who greeted him with his customary good will, although this time a little frozen with immobility. But what was most extraordinary was that by reason of his grandeur called majestuous—another way (he soon noticed), no less miserable, of ending up removed from space—he had to be aware of the impeded speech that henceforth, like a grave profoundly opened around him, a failure of words in words, seemed destined to preserve his isolation. Who was responsible for it? Must he linger over such a thing happening? Should he, speaking of it to him, confiding it to him as an element of their relationship and perhaps a sign of life, sign of death, risk lessening its importance? As discretion necessarily meant saying everything in advance, how could he, in the game of their discreet silence, introduce this new indiscretion that claimed, in some form, by some wild muteness, to modify the course of what had been said? Impeded speech that found its equivalent in silent ease, inexorable, leaving room only for the continuous murmur of the river crossing the room between the immobile hills. Ease as of a thing already written and nevertheless always still to be written and always not writing itself. "There you are—this time it's you—sovereign over speech."—"For the benefit of age." According to his conviction, the monumental character that was suddenly visible, that of a dead sovereignty, of a name sovereignly alive, vicissitudes that attracted them towards one another, in a deep past, placing them on the plateaux of a powerful scale, was also meant to make material, by contrast, what lightness there would be in this coming that no one had any intention— or perhaps only episodically—of marking in the present in saying, murmur held by a flowing speech: they're coming, they arrive, since speech rebounded, as from brink to brink, from past to past. Which did not stop them, in their elegant shyness, freer every day, from denying us our own discourse about them in reducing us to this solemn, venerable manifestation.*

♦ The power to name the neuter was, as always, the power not to name it, to dedicate to it, from closer and closer, all language, all that is visible and all that is invisible of language, and yet to withdraw it from language precisely by this donation that reduces the neuter to being only the recipient of its own message. As if the dusk where night and day seem to trade places, in favor of a darkness that illuminates and of a clarity that dissipates itself, in an indifferent equality, were not the interval impossible to fill up, nor the difference always previously marked, out of which there could be an eternal day, an eternal night, and their perpetual exchange.

♦ *The City, always alive, animated, imperturbable, completely foreign to the idea that one could die in it: yet, in this room in which he was seated, dreamy, I crossed it, as one passes distractedly over the graves in a cemetery.*

♦ The neuter can be named, since it is named (even if this is not a proof). But what is designated by this name? The desire to dominate the neuter, a desire to which the neuter immediately lends itself, all the more so as it is foreign to any domination and as it has always already marked, with its passive insistance, the desire that thus infects its object and every object with it.

♦    *What frightened us was the point to which they needed us, needed our ignorance, our disappearance, our ardent complicity, that of a dead thing signalling to them and attracting them.*

♦    Grafted on to every word: the neuter

♦    *It is as if he had said to him, saying it in such a friendly way: friendship withdraws from us.*

♦    *Entwined, separated, witnesses without testimony, coming towards us, coming toward one another also, in the detour of time that they were called upon to make turn.*

♦    *Immobile, stricken with dignity, as one would be stricken with death, inclining slowly toward one another, as one inclines to greet another (greeting thought), we were awaiting our common fall.*

♦    That this was impossible did not prevent a mere nothing's being required for it to be produced—but precisely a mere nothing.

For such a long time, we had been preparing ourselves to celebrate the event which, now that it was coming, there was no longer time, so that we were not yet ready and so that it was not coming anyway.

♦    *While he went to his daily appointment, knowing, with a knowledge from the depths of the ages, that he was seated, or perhaps leaning towards the large, heavy marble table, while at the same time, from the other side, the strange man—the man whom he had not decided in what terms it would be appropriate to call to—remained dreamy and with nothing that might change the vision of him, he was startled to hear him speak with his usual voice, clear, neuter, so that one would have had to say that it stressed and cut off every word, if what it said so clearly had not failed to correspond to any particular word. "It's the impeded speech, he said to reassure himself, a long animal sob"; but he had, indeed, to admit that he could not get himself out of it so easily, since everything invited him to save the triumphant affirmation that came to him by way of his stammering. It was to confirm it to him that the other one offered him his hand, as usual, faithfully, in a friendly way, saying: "Pardon me, I didn't recognize you." Yes, this was said in such a convincing way that there was nothing left to do but torment himself by not believing it.*

♦     *The room, shrunken or immense, according to the time the words took to cross it and to come back to him; sometimes he said to himself: they will not come back.*

♦     Let us admit—in a way that is all the more pressing since we cannot admit it, arbitrarily then, with the shameless beauty of the arbitrary—, let us admit that the neuter does not belong to the language of the living, and without belonging to the language the dead do not speak, would constitute the only word, perhaps because there is no other, which would have come to us from the border region, infinite, where the silence of some, the silence of others, skirt one another, although no translation between them is possible because of their absolute identity, no less than because of their absolute difference. So that it is not heard on either side, but only murmured or borrowed—and perhaps one must say that it is the people of the dead who would repeat it with the most reticence, certainly not because it would be a nostalgic echo of the world of the living (nothing living in it), but because, listening to it, they might learn that there is something more dead than death.

◆     Dead desire: desire immutably changed into desire through death and death as an adjective.

◆     *. . . begging to receive what had always been given him (winning over the complaints, the sighs, the murmurs that all escaped from him).*
To beg: to beg thought, to refine it to the point that it crumbles.

◆     How can it be that one speaks, speaking, thus? The idea of losing what one does not have, days, nights, then of losing this loss, awkwardly known as death. To lose the ability to lose is not, by the play of the negative, to have, but rather, and not even, to attain non–power in some form that inscribes itself against any form.

◆     *Listening, not to the words, but to the suffering that endlessly, from one word to the next, runs through words.*

◆     *"What would we do if we were forbidden to do anything?"—"What we do now, but to such a degree of inaction that the prohibition would fall away on its own."*

◆     *"I speak so that you don't have to speak, and, nevertheless, so that no one suspects you of being deprived of speech— but all this unintentionally."*

86

♦     *Even without being resolved to it, they advanced towards what withdrew any certainty from them with a grandiose assurance.*

♦     The impeded speech: the speech that returns to us from muteness without passing through the assuaging of silence.

♦     *". . . innocent, you alone have the right to call yourself innocent."—"If I have the right, as I believe, I am not innocent, innocence is without right."*

♦     *There where we were without fear, without suffering, without desire, because of this given over to perpetual fear, desire and suffering.*

♦     *Speaking to him while he slept, it was in a deep sleep— sleep seeking sleep—, that he asked for an answer: and the answer, each time, was the waking of this friend.*

♦     *He does not renounce living, he only closes his eyes.*

♦     Who says: breath of nothingness, would never dare say: truth of the neuter or knowledge of the neuter,—this simply because language, in saying it, would experience the brilliance of a victorious language.

♦     All that is crude in the crudely repeated affirmation by which the anonymous tries to reach us, there where we would be placed outside of the game by the relation of inaccessibility that the morcellating demand of writing, like the fiction of this badly unified word death, seems to hold by default, takes on all its caricatural strength when a writer receives from his disappearance a new energy and the glamour of renown. This second immortality exalts his weakness, the power he no longer has (power always usurped from his living self), to be still behind his work to defend it, to defend himself in it, to make himself illustrious in its shadow and hold it in the advantageous light that is appropriate to it. The author dead, the work appears to live from this death. The author was superfluous. At present, this superfluity, until then dissimulated (the author, however decided he was about losing himself in the impersonality of the book, did not stop speaking, speaking, sometimes indirectly, about his book), takes on this character of a lack which, fortunately or necessarily, calls for commentary, the desire of others to make themselves the author of this authorless work, ironically given over by its solitude to the interest of "all". But the superfluousness, once sadly or joyously represented by the author, soon finds itself again at work in the work "in person", which is always superfluous as well, not only in regard to the indefinite series of works already written in which it always necessarily takes its place, by a surplus necessity, but also in relation to itself, as if all that it lacked could only inscribe itself outside of the work, which does not exist. Whence the appeal to a morcellating, repetitive demand: the three knocks of the traditional theater that would seem to announce that something is going to happen, while instead they reverberate in the eternal empty tomb.


◆     The work, after death, is sent, like the dove of Arche, to give recognition to that which has survived, in carrying back the branch green with meaning, and it comes back—it always comes back, perhaps once or twice—, changed, by the return, into the dove of before the flood, antediluvian.

♦     He who speaks does not, through speech, have a relation to being nor in consequence to the present of being: thus he did not speak.


♦     *What torments you, poor word that no one pronounces, except by mistake?*


♦     *Dying as if to verify that he was dying.*


♦     To repeat what one has not heard and what has not been said: to repeat this also—and to stop suddenly, pretending to see in this the essence of repetition.


♦     If writing, dying, are words that would be close to one another through the distance in which they arrange themselves, both incapable of any present, it is clear that one cannot be satisfied with simple phrases putting into play simple relations that are also too immediately pathetic to maintain their relational character—phrases like these: when you speak, it is already death that speaks, or: you die writing and dying you write; all formulations destined to show what is almost laughable in carelessly manipulating unequal terms, without the medium of silence or the long preparation of a tacit development or, even better, without eliminating their temporal character. (And yet our culture lives on these simple relations, only reversed: the idea of immortality assured by the work, or the idea that to write is to preserve oneself from death, thus to keep it in reserve, or the idea that the death of the writer would liberate the work in casting a new light on it, a light of shadow, and so on, the work always suspected of being the life of death itself.) Dying, writing, do not take place, there where someone generally dies, where someone generally writes.

One must thus erase, withdraw the word death in dying, like speech in writing. Speech evokes death too naturally, too immediately. To speak is to lose rather than to retain; to entrust to forgetfulness rather than to memory; to give up breath (to run out of breath) rather than to breathe. To speak, in this sense, an ironic sense, is indeed to have the last word, to have it in order no longer to have it: to speak with this last word that nobody pronounces or takes up as the last. From which it results—and it is the beginning of a very long and ancient certainty—that writing seems invented to make more lasting what does not last or to prevent this loss of speech that is still speech from being lost: in other words, writing, essentially conservative, would mark, in assuring the safeguard and identity of marks. Will one answer that it is then a matter of a second writing, the one which agrees in following speech, by tranquil temporal succession and repose in books, to conserve speech? One can say this, on condition that one also says that writing is always second in the sense that, even if nothing precedes it, it does not pose as first, instead ruining all primacy through an indefinite reference that leaves no place even for the void. Such is, then, barely indicated, the dispersed violence of writing, a violence by which speech is always already set apart, effaced in advance and no longer restored, violence, it is true, that is not natural and that also prevents us, dying, from dying a natural death.

◆　Past, future, neither was ever given; what has been as unforeseeable as what will be. Death, this badly unified word, interrogation always displaced.

◆　*Words had meaning only because meaning, introducing suspicion, filtering, invisible vapor, harmful, from a place without origin, did not cease, even in seeming to give them life, to break up, to mortify, words.*

♦     When we say: it is madness, or, more seriously, he is mad, to say this is already madness.

♦     *Fear, fear of the fear that is produced by nothing in particular, except nights without sleep, days without wakefulness, desire for that which provokes the fear that nothing provokes.*

♦     *He speaks the truth, otherwise he thinks he would go mad, but he does not notice—or only too late—that the truth is that he is mad. This mad truth, he closes his mouth so as not to have to speak it, hoping—this is what is frightening—all the same to remain in the true without saying anything.*

♦     *Immobile before this unmoving friend, still he is never immobile enough; the feeling of a threat comes from this, and the fear—the fear that nothing provokes; one of the two moves, it is not completely life; one goes to get up perhaps, it will be night, the other will continue to mount guard with these vacillating words.*

♦     *"You torment yourself in speaking."—"If not, I would torment myself in not speaking."*

♦     *While they waited on the threshold, far away, yet perhaps already leaning towards us, and watching us as if we were a single thing, he saw, falling over the face of the young girl, as the night falls, the dark hair that completely hides it.*

♦     *"We speak, we speak, two immobile men whom immobility maintains facing one another, the only ones to speak, the*

*last to speak."—"Do you mean that from now on we speak*
*because our words are without consequence, without effect, a*
*stammering from the depths of the ages?"—"Stay calm, look*
*how I'm calm."—"You're not calm, you're afraid as I'm afraid,*
*fear makes us majestuous, solemn."—"Solemn, majestuous."*


♦    If we could, through a reduction or a preliminary dissi-
dence, separate death and dying, speech and writing, we
would obtain, although at great expense and at great pains, a
sort of theoretical calm, theoretical happiness, this calm and
this happiness that we grant, at the bottom of their happy
tomb, to the great dead—the dead are always momentarily
great—who are also, and par excellence, the marking figures
or supports of the theory. This badly ordered network—the
entanglement of speech and writing—cannot be cut apart except on condition that it be restored each time and made even
more difficult to disentangle by the practice (impracticable,
sovereign, blind, piteous, in every case) of writing, that knows
only after the fact, only ever knowing it with a borrowed
knowledge, that the knot is cut by it, although it was not yet
tied, and that it is this decisive violence of practice alone that
makes a gordian knot. It is thus this cutting, preliminary
violence of writing, that assures, extremely ironic effect, the
unity of writing-speech in allowing us to read it in these two
terms (like an open book, with a text said to be a translation
on one side, and a text called original on the other, without
one's even being able to decide which side is which, nor even if
it is a question of a text in two versions, so much do identity
and difference cover one another up)—duality that it un-
makes and remakes each time in giving rise to a more artful
speech.
    Speech is artful, in proportion to its weakness, its ability
to efface itself, all the more itself the more it impedes itself,
held back to the point of stammering, (nobody would look for it
from speech specialists; it is more "natural" for it than for
writing not to have any relation to beauty, to the good: "he is a
beautiful speaker"; while "he who writes well" is only the heir

of "he who speaks well"; value judgements come to writing in as much as, substitute for speech, writing completes and fulfills it). In this way, one would say, still living and even failing in order to be as close as possible to life that never shines more brilliantly than at the moment of losing itself. But the moribund speech (speech not dying, but of dying itself) has perhaps always already passed the limit that life does not pass: passing unbeknownst to it by the route that writing has traced out in marking it as untracable.

♦    Let us suppose that dying is not illuminated by that which seems to give it meaning, being-dead. Death, being-dead, certainly unsettle us, but as a gross or inert event (the thing itself) or even as the reversal of meaning, the being of what is not, the painful non-meaning that is, nevertheless, always taken up again by meaning, there where, in its heavy and reassuring way, the power of being continues to dominate. After all, "being dead" is able to make the word death take the attributive position, like one of the memorable attributes of being, only a disconcerting sign of the omnipotence of being that still always governs non-being. But dying, no more than it *cannot* finish or accomplish itself, even in death, does not let itself be situated or affirmed in a relation of life, even as a declining relation, a declining of life. Dying does not localize itself in an event, nor does it last in the way of a temporal becoming; dying does not last, does not end, and, prolonging itself in death, tears this away from the state of a thing in which it would like to retreat peacefully. It is dying, the error of dying without completion, that makes the dead one suspect and death unverifiable, withdrawing from it in advance the benefit of an *event*. And life knows nothing of dying, says nothing about it, without, however, confining itself to silence; there is, suddenly and always, a murmur among words, the rumor of absence that passes in and to the outside of discourse, a non-silent arrest that intervenes, there where the noise of writing, order of the somber curator, maintains an interval for dying, while dying, the interval itself perhaps, cannot take place in it. Dying: that which does not rely on life; but it is also death that prevents us from dying.


◆     If the worklessness of the neuter is at work somewhere, you will not find it in the thing that is dead, but there where without life without death without time without duration the drop by drop of dying falls: noise too strident to let itself be heard: that which murmurs in the resounding burst, that which stammers at the height of beautiful speech.


◆     *The words did not communicate themselves, did not know themselves, playing among themselves according to the limits of near and far and the unknown decisions of difference.*


◆     Dying, in this sense, does not have the crushing solidity of non-being, the irrevocability of what has happened, of being in the past. It is nothing more than a simulacrum, something that pretends and pretends to efface itself in effacing us. The "pretending," the disintegration of dying, it is that which, at each instant outside of the instant, parallel with the sinuous line of life, makes us slip along a perversely straight path.


◆     To die: as if we only died in the infinitive. To die: the reflection in the mirror perhaps, the mirroring of an absence of figure, less the image of someone or something that was not there than an effect of invisibility, touching on nothing profound and only too superficial to let itself be grasped or even recognized. As if the invisible distributed itself in filigree, without the distribution of points of visibility being there for anything, thus not in the intimacy of the design, but too much on the outside, in an exteriority of being of which being bears no marks.

94

◆ The proverbial formula: "as soon as someone begins to live, he is old enough to die," is indeed impressive in as much as it distributes mortal possibility uncertainly the whole length of life, in an unexpected relation with duration. All the same, through this formula, there is still a facile relation between life and death: dying remains a possibility—a power that life attributes to itself or that is verified in it and confirms itself in death—determined in this way between two terms (one begins to die with this beginning that is life's debut—the expulsion of birth being metaphorically recovered as an overwhelming encounter with a sort of death—, and one ends by that which finishes life, cadaveric equality or, to go further to the ultimate repose, the entropic equality of the universe). But perhaps dying has no determined relation to living, to the reality, the presence of "life". A pure fantasy perhaps, a mockery that no trace would make material in the present, or again a madness that would overwhelm being from top to bottom and, at the same time, would only reach us as an imperceptible neurosis, escaping any observation, invisible because too visible. Thus perhaps to write: a writing that would not be a possibility of speech (no more than dying is a possibility of life)—a murmur nonetheless, a madness nonetheless that would play at the silent surface of language.

◆ Dying (the non-arrival of what comes about), the prohibited mocking the prohibition, there where it would be, in some way, forbidden to die and thus where dying, without ever coming to a resolute act of transgression, would disperse in its indecision (dying being essentially indecisive) the moment infinitely divided by it due to which, if this moment reassembled itself, it would be necessary to die outside the law and always clandestinely.

◆ *Among the people of the dead passes the shudder of the rumor: it is forbidden to die.*

♦     The death that is sudden, proper, optative: that which acquits dying.


♦     The work of mourning: the inverse of dying.


♦     The death that strikes in the fullness of life, as in a place removed from the movement of dying (a death without dying): analytic, as from a practice that would separate the inseparable, writing-speech. But dying was already invisible there, yet nowhere, without effect, without relation to this suddeness that is death's own, even if it is slow.


♦     The unforeseeability of death, the invisibility of dying.


♦     The unique blow of repetitive death. If death takes place only once, it is because dying, reiterating itself endlessly through its essential unaccomplishment, the accomplishment of the unaccomplished, repeats itself, without this repetition being numbered and without this number being numbered, like a beating heart whose every beat would be illicit, unnumbered.


♦     "It is forbidden to die," we hear this in ourselves constantly, not as an appeal to the obligation of life, but as the voice of death itself, breaking the prohibition each time (as if all too clear to the one who, giving himself death, dies forbidden).

Perhaps one punishes the act of killing all the more decidedly as one cannot reach, much less sanction, the imperceptible movement of death. To kill, to kill oneself: like a right over dying. But the horror of the death camps, of those dying by the thousands, suddenly and unceasingly called out, numbered, identified, makes each dying person guilty of his death that was never more innocent and condemns him to *dying* of the very abjection of *death,* in making appear, through a major indiscretion, what should not let itself be seen.

Where is the event of death? Where the obscurity of dying? Like two speeches never pronounced that, boringly repetitive and frightening, would resonate only at the moment—at each moment—of the collapse of every language.

♦    "I die not dying" does not only express the mortal desire that arises, as unrealizable, from death's attraction: it lets us foresee the movement of dying, its incessant and simultaneous redoubling, in a relation that eats away, of different signs, in which the game of difference mortally plays itself out. Dying of not dying dramatizes, makes shine for an instant, through the paradox of the formulation, the impossibility of maintaining in a solely affirmative or solely negative position the difference that carries the word death.

♦    *Dying—dying in the cold and dissolution of the Outside: always outside oneself as outside life.*

♦    Suicide, temptation of defiance so prolonged and so clear (too clear) that it seems difficult—almost embarrassing—to resist it. Act of transgression: the prohibition not pronounced by a law or by "nature", but by the mortal indecisiveness of the act itself, this prohibition broken as soon as affirmed, transgression accomplished at the same time as suppressed, and the passage of transgression—the "not beyond" [*le "pas au-delà"*], there where nevertheless one does not pass—dangerously symbolized, offered in the name of "personal representation": the trespassed, one would say. Act unhoped for (without hope) of unifying the duplicity of death and of reunifying in one time, through a decision of impatience, the eternal repetitions of that which, dying, does not die. Then, the temptation to name, in attributing it to oneself, the anonymous, that which is spoken only in the third person and in the neuter. Or again the power to enlarge, as if in proportion to it, in localizing it and dating it, the infinitely small of death, that which always escapes—all this in exaltation, fatigue, unhappiness, fear, uncertainty, all movements that end up covering up the *indiscretion* of such an act, however obviously and essentially committed: ambiguous refusal to submit oneself to the requirement of dying silently and discreetly. Respecting silence in the act of being quiet. The *impossibility* of suicide is alone able to attenuate the frightful indiscretion: as if one had pretended to pretend, there in broad daylight, but in a light such that, despite its ostentation, nobody sees anything, nobody knows anything of what happens.

♦      Dying, like the hand that not far from the paper would hold itself immobile without writing anything or would even move ahead without tracing anything (perhaps because what it writes will be revealed only later by the unrefined processes of the sympathetic ink).

♦      Dying, in the discretion that this word attributes to itself in distinguishing itself from the obviousness, the visibility of death, makes itself in turn extremely visible, like an entity (Dying) dissimulating its capitalized form that illness, aging, help us to reveal; like the effect of a reactive or of a reheating—the fever of life. Dying of an illness or of old age, we do not die only ill, old, but deprived of or frustrated by what would seemingly be secret in dying itself: thus reduced to not dying.

98

◆    No defiance perhaps in the defiance by which we would give ourselves death, gift always undeserved, but only this unnoticed defiance that any desire supposes, the attraction without attraction which, all of a sudden and in spite of us (no, *I* do not desire to die), illuminates and burns, consuming, ravaging the secret patience—the obstinance—of dying, and betraying the unrevealed, the undesirable desire that the movement of death would carry (without carrying us to dying and more in the form of a refusal, of an infinite anxiety that the thought of the final falling due vainly makes concrete).


◆    The vulgarity or obscenity (the bad omen) of death: its lack of circumspection that comes from its *exposition,* that is, from that which makes it, in spite of everything, public: given up to morcellating, to the dissolution of the Outside—that which, by an association that is difficult to avoid, difficult to accept, tends to let mortal innocence and sexual innocence be thought together in their reciprocal inappropriateness, in the perversion that "is appropriate" to one and the other (perversion of what is never correct), in the modesty that this perversion requires or rejects (while still requiring it); both of them are things, things called dirty and decomposing themselves through a plurality that would be more dirty than every dirty thing (but plurality immediately taken back, obfuscated— how otherwise?—while we pursue our work of unification in the necessity of speaking and of thinking sexuality as a unity of sexual things—all that runs, rends itself, undoes itself, without any personal property or appropriation—and death as the unity of mortal effects). What is left is that the passivity of death makes appear, in contrast, all that remains of action, of impulse, of living play in sexual diversion or expenditure: we do not enjoy death in dying even if we desire it, while desire, in sexual play, even if it is mortal, and even if it separates itself from any *jouissance* and makes it impossible, still promises us and gives us the movement of dying as that which may be re*jouissance—jouissance*[9] infinitely repeated— of life, at its *expense.*

♦ We expose death hurriedly, we bury it hurriedly, hiding what we have shown at once, as if under the pressure of a publicization or the demand of a definitive bringing to light. Death is always public, it asks to be publicized, thus completed and holding us free of it once we have identified the unidentifiable: whence these mocking ceremonies to which the public hurries because it is a part of them, as it is itself a part of what is publicized in them, in a public sovereignty in which it recognizes itself in enchanting itself, in lamenting itself, conscious, busy, mortally agitated, participating in every way (even if it takes no part in them) in these funerary rites and at once affirming its right: obsequies.

♦ *On the threshold, coming from the outside perhaps, the two young names like two figures behind the glass about whom we could not say for sure whether they are inside or outside, since no one, except the two figures, who expect everything from us, could say where we are.*

♦ *When he would resume his walking, getting up once more to cross the room and go before them, he would be called to at once, would come back at once, would sit down in order to answer more easily and would notice that he had never stopped being immobile; there would remain the terrified feeling of the return.*

♦ *Thank you for all these words that have not been spoken.*

♦ Knowing uses our strength, but not knowing exhausts it.

100

♦    Transgression does not transgress the law, it carries it away with it.

♦    *Night, still more nocturnal, more foreign to the night: the night of words. Where are you going, you in the lack of night?*

♦    To no longer be able, such that after these words one could no longer even know what one is no longer able to do.

♦    To write, when one is no longer able to live, is not even as absurd as to write that in these conditions one feels this. Each is given the right to add a codicil at the very last moment.

The very last moment, this fluttering of a heart that no longer beats to life.

The very last moment, we would, writing this word, vainly have felt all the fraudulence there is in writing it, even if we add that it does not belong to the moments, that it is thus not the very last—yet (must we then thank you for this "yet", supplementary word that nothing follows this time, except, except this pure gratitude?)

♦    *"There is no more fraudulence here than before; we are speaking of the last moment, precisely because it prevents us from speaking, even if we have not been speaking of it for a long time."*

♦    If death, by way of capricious falling dues, magnifies the dead person, is it not for this convenient reason that the latter's silence, having passed, from now on, from the inside to the outside, sollicits a forceful public speech that each one feels he has the right to make heard: the right to speak in the dead one's place, through a right of deputeeship that is delegated to him and of which he acquits himself, making his own eulogy in this eulogy, assuring his survival, the survival of speech, in advance: eulogy, the good speech, which says only, repeating it, alas.

◆    *He slept the sleep that demands attention, precisely because nothing can any longer interrupt it.*

◆    A hoax, no doubt, final hoax, the deception of what is supplementary, of what adds itself with no right at the end, "sovereignty"—yes, all that can be said, but on condition that we think that such a lure comes to us from death, that great misleader, so deceitful that we deceive ourselves again in qualifying it as such.

◆    *The more he encloses himself, the more he says that he belongs to the Outside.*

◆    *Attempt to delimit a certain territory again with the absence of any limit.*

◆    But the deception of the public death (that which makes the mocking presence sublime, which exalts what is no longer there, makes a gift to all of loss itself) is already at work in the simulacrum of dying, the insinuation and the perfidy by which we are summoned: "you die, and yet you do not die, and yet you die."

102

◆ *Dread, dread there anew, he had to write this word that did not let him write anything else, and not even this word, all of a sudden forbidden, unpronounceable, so excessive that there was nothing in his life vast enough, vain enough, to contain it, and so he had—there was the catch—to enlarge this life even to the false consciousness that he was not living, that he was dying.*

◆ *There was something like a word that could not be pronounced, even when one succeeded in saying it and perhaps precisely because one had, at every instant, and as if there were not enough instants for the purpose, to say it, to think it.*

◆ *One can write it once, live it once: even if strictly, and as if inadvertently, one could in a unique way reach madness— what happens when madness comes back a second time? One would have the right to think oneself better defended, facing a more familiar adversary, with whose tricks, with whose atrocious contact, with whose weaknesses, also, one is familiar (what a strange familiarity). However, one thinks only of this one thing: what had been impossible—madness—even in the memory one retains of it, is possible again, and what had once been possible, the grace of liberating oneself, is now the impossible, the more so as one could not appeal to it for the same help (one is allowed to have been weak one day; weakness that is repeated, even if it is unhappiness that is repeated in it, does not deserve any respect). What is left? Once again the extreme possibility, that which is offered by madness for one to defend oneself against it, and on which it has placed its mark—a forbidden possibility? certainly, but is not madness, which was not less forbidden, also there, without right, not freeing from all legitimacy, but condemning every life, every death to a sup-*plementary *illegitimacy?*

♦    If writing, dying are in relation to one another, relation always broken in this relation and still more shattered as soon as a writing would pretend to affirm it (but it affirms nothing, it only writes, it does not even write), it is because, under the influence of the same deceit (which, deceiving on all sides, is never the same), these words enter into resonnance. And one can then enumerate affirmations in order: one can say that the book is to writing what death would be to the movement of dying; one can say that writing, dying are what are most discreet, although always made known by the public Last Act, the great tomblike rock of the Book, the sovereign publication of absent presence; one can say that dying, writing, without falling under the prohibition already pronounced by a law, both have to do with a prohibition that cannot be promulgated, as with an empty transgression. Obscure center of fallacious relations. We do not die offending, no more than we write guilty; nevertheless, there is a rupture there that the term finitude illuminates badly and of which religious myths make us overly conscious. Dying is a "law of nature", and yet we do not die naturally. We cannot do otherwise, and this necessity about which we are sure without believing in it (always surprised, at the final moment, by the unbelievable), puts the mask of infidelity, eyes closed, on each of our faces: we abandon ourselves, we abandon those to whom we should not be absent, we abandon "life", and that by a sort of distraction, as if, had we been more attentive, we could have avoided the inevitable. However, it is certainly more than a betrayal: it is a false betrayal. All is falsified, when dying comes into play; even error is a lure, failure that finally fails nothing and that does not fail life, which always takes advantage of it. The same for writing, perhaps, form which, by another lure, the movement of dying proposes to us as a compensation, a detour of illusion, finally, the trap: as if, writing, we have to die supplementarily, and more unjustified, with a supplementary loss of innocence that is itself innocent, but which involves us in becoming responsible for the movement of dying—transgression that transgresses nothing.

♦    This character of prohibiting without prohibition: becoming more and more visible even to this singularity in which it denounces itself in madness.

*Dread always and everywhere guilty, and, from this fact, unconcerned.*


♦    These peculiarities distributed the length of a perversely straight line, to die, to go mad, to write. Dying lets us understand: a normal anomaly; the rule, irregularity itself; and not an exception to the rule but, in as much as regular, that which could not appertain to a law. It happens, in certain societies, that those who let death—the thing—be seen in dying, which is unreality, leave or are deported out of the territory: social exclusion banishes, in accusing it, the obscene transgression, even the fact that henceforth the anomaly, ceasing to dissimulate itself, appears, or again that what shows itself is indecisiveness itself, about which one must decide by exclusion. The dead are not good company, but are at once reclaimed by the rites: the great funeral ceremonies, the minute rules of protocol, mourning, always collective and always public, establishes them in a social site, even if it is set apart: cemetery, myth, family or legendary history, religion of the dead. Mortal indecisiveness has no place, nor any mitigating status. Even when dying seems to fill the being to the point that we call it, not without difficulty, a dying one, we do not know, facing the indecisive strangeness, what it expects from us who are there, idle, close to the place where chance plays, spectators to non-presence, touched in our most intimate loyalty: our relation, in ourselves, to a subject. And, in conformity with the customs of the day, we bustle about doing nothing, we help the living one, we help him to die, but we do not help dying, something accomplishes itself there, in every absence and by default, which does not accomplish itself, something that would be the "step not/beyond" that does not belong to duration, that repeats itself endlessly and that separates us (witnesses to what escapes witnessing) from any appropriateness as from any relation to an I, subject of a Law.

And we can easily understand and say that the silent speech, this infinite murmur, thus also pronounces itself in us, that we die with the one who dies, as he dies in our place, in the place where we think that we sojourn—not dying because we lose a part of common life, but rather because it is "dying", intransitive loss, that we share with him, in a movement of pure passivity that passion without tears sometimes seems to assume. This we can say, and no doubt rightly. Still, nothing is said, if we do not force ourselves to think that which even the evidence of agony does not reveal, the invisible rupture of prohibition, the transgression to which we feel we are accessories, because it is also our own strangeness: something overwhelming, but also completely shocking. In the narrow space where this is accomplished without being accomplished, there is no longer any law, nor society, nor alliance, nor union—and yet nothing free, nothing safe: only beneath the appearance of a devastating violence and of a suffering that extinguishes itself, a secret that is not spoken, an unknown word that bears silence away with it.

♦ *"I do not know, but I know that I am going to have known":* thus dying speaks through the suffering silence of the dying one.

♦ *A hand that extends itself, that refuses itself, that we cannot take hold of in any way.*

♦ Empty transgression, image of the movement of every transgression that nothing prohibited precedes, but which also does not place the limit by the crossing of the uncrossable. Neither before, nor during, nor after. It is as in another region, the other of any region. In the day's domain reigns the law, the forbidden that it pronounces, the possible and the speech that justifies. In the nocturnal space, there are violations of the law, the violence that breaks the prohibition, the non-possible, the silence that refuses what is just. Transgression belongs neither to the day nor to the night. Never does it encounter the law that is nevertheless everywhere. Transgression: the inevitable accomplishment of what is *impossible* to accomplish—and this would be dying itself.

"It is forbidden."—"It is inevitable."—"Still, always to be avoided according to the movement of duration and as if there were no present moment appropriate for the falling due."—"From this comes the need, without justification, to have always to gain an extra moment, a supplement of time, not for life, but for dying that does not produce itself in time."—"Dying defers, without asking for a delay, nor, failing the delay, letting itself be marked by an offense; stranger also to this future present that retains time as a succession of presents."—"You die and yet you do not die and yet: thus, in a time without present, the dying that defers speaks to you."—"Perhaps again according to the demand of the return: that will always take place, because that has always already taken place."—"As if dying let us in some way *live* in the eternal detour of a past and the eternal detour of a future that no present would unify."—"To die is not declined."—"This inert infinitive, agitated by an infinite neutrality that could not coincide with itself, infinitive without present."—"So that one could affirm: it is forbidden to die *in the present*."—"Which also means: the present does not die, and there is no present for dying. It is the present that would in some way pronounce the prohibition."—"While the transgression of dying, which has always already broken with present time, comes to substitute, in the unaccomplishment proper to it, for the trinary duration that the predominance of the present unifies, the time of difference in which this would always take place because it has always already happened: dying, coming again."—"The prohibition remains intact: one does not die in the present."—"It remains intact. But, in as much as it is the present that pronounces it and in which the transgression is unaccomplished in a future-past time, removed from any affirmation of presence, the transgression has always already withdrawn the present time of its pronouncement from the prohibition: has prevented it or prohibited it in dislocating it."—"Thus a time without present would be 'affirmed', according to the demand of the return."—"This is why even transgression does not accomplish itself."

♦     Dying in the multiple doubling of what does not take place in the present. One does not die alone, and if it is humanly so necessary to be the fellow man of the one who dies, it is, although in a mocking way, in order to share roles, to alleviate dying of this prohibition that awaits it in leaving to it the attainment of the immobile transgression. We hold back the dying one by the most gentle of prohibitions: do not die now, for there is no now for dying. Not, the ultimate word, the defense that pleads its case, the stammering negative: not— you will die.

♦     If the prohibition "thou shalt not kill" is written only on tablets already broken, it is because it makes the Law predominant all of a sudden in substituting for the impossible encounter with the forbidden and the transgression the affirmation of a successive time (according to a before and after) where there is first prohibition, then recognition of prohibition, then refusal by the guilty rupture. What do the broken tablets signify? Perhaps the shattering of dying, the interruption of the present that dying has always introduced into time beforehand. "Thou shalt not kill" obviously means: "do not kill he who will die in any case" and means: "because of that, do not infringe on dying, do not decide the indecisive, do not say: this is done, claiming for yourself a right over this 'not yet'; do not pretend that the last word has been spoken, time completed, the Messiah come at last."

♦     Thought, death: one sometimes quicker than the other, sometimes the former, the infinitely small, more diminished than the latter, the infinitely small, both outside the present, falling into the void of the future, the void of the past.

♦    We can ask ourselves about the neuter, knowing that the interrogation does not go beyond interrogation; this would already be neutralized, and "what?" cannot be its form, even if it then leaves the place of the questioned void in questioning only this empty place; maybe because the neuter always comes into the question that is out of the question. We can always ask ourselves about the neuter, without the neuter entering into the questioning. As for the response, the repeated echo of the neuter, it is not even pure tautology, since it disperses the speech of the same. *The neuter, the neuter:* is it a repetition, or something like the ricochets which, to infinity, by the slipping of that which slips, decline multiple series: the pebble, propulsion, the surface that carries, the surface that hides itself, time the straightness that bends and makes a return up to the fall that results, without being a part of them, from all these moments and thus cannot be isolated, even in taking place apart, in such a way that the singular point that would mark it, remains, in its singularity, outside the reality of the whole: unreal and unrealized?

♦    *Each of us awaits the speech that would authorize it: "Yes, you can do it."—"I can't do it."—"Then what are you waiting for?"—"I am waiting for what I do not desire."— "There is no speech that would authorize; all that authorizes concerns life; you are thus authorized to live."*

♦    Dying without authority, as suits the one who usurps the name of author and, not ceasing to die, without continuity and without end, authorizes himself to defer dying.
Dying defers, without one's deferring to die.
Dying does not authorize dying.

109

♦ *"Now, you can do it."—"Then I can no longer do it."—*
*"Now does not pass, it maintains itself."—"Now grows smaller*
*each time you pronounce it, always smaller and more fragile*
*than your speech or your thought."—"Go then from threshold*
*to threshold, poor dying."*

♦ Dying's difficulty comes in part from the fact that we think it only in the future and that, thinking it in the past, we immobilize it in the form of death. Dying in the past would be being dead. Or else the past of dying would be this weightiness that would make death yet to come, always more heavy, more bereft of a future. As if dying lasted and, finally, as it is useless to denounce the illusion of it, lived, doublet of the word to live. Only, and immediately, we feel that these two series are not correlative: perhaps because dying, in its repetitive singularity, does not form a true series, or, on the contrary, forms only one series, while living escapes serial dispersion, in appealing always to a whole, a living all, the living presence of the all of life.

The demand of the return, impossible to think, empty future, empty past, helps us to welcome (in the impossibility of thinking it) that which could be the always already completed of dying, that which passes without traces and that one has always to await from the infinite void of the future, wait excluded from the present that would be only the double fall into the abyss, or the double abyss of the fall, or, to speak more soberly, the duplicity of difference. To die, to come again.

♦ To die too light, lighter than any fantasy in its phantasmatic heaviness.

♦ To die according to the lightness of dying and not by the anticipated heaviness of death—the dead weight of the dead thing—, would be to die in relation to some immortality.

110

♦ *Transgression, this lightness of immortal dying.*

♦ Haunting obsession, to bring dying back to itself, as in crossing the city, one leads the passerby back to his passage. Dying in this return to dying. There is no guardian of dying.

♦ The house haunted the phantoms: here and there, a threshold where there was no ground.

♦ *They would come, going from threshold to threshold, looking for us, letting themselves be looked for, the young names.*

♦ *"Don't forget that we don't have to do anything in order for them to come."—"Nothing in order for them not to come."—"Not look for them."—"Not flee from them."—"That is too symmetrical: you can, without looking for them, without fleeing from them, still direct your will so that the chances of a meeting are not of your making: avoid them so that the inevitable remains obscure."—"There is not a will more general than my will that could make me suspect that I substitute myself for it: it is like a necessity attracting and repelling, but always attracting, a necessity whose attraction it would be given to me, without proper proceedings and without even a wait, to recognize."—"Attraction by which, keeping us in the mystery of the illusion, we think we recognize them, name them, keep them at a distance under the brilliance of the name, and thus, embellishing it, facilitate their approach."—"Always too close for them to be near to us."—"And yet separated by the movement of their coming."—"They're not coming."*

♦ *The words exchanged over the heavy marble table, going from immobility to immobility. They would separate them-*

*selves by several steps, listening to the young murmur of the days and years below. All around, there were men apparently sleeping, lying on the very ground, covers thrown over them like one throws earth onto an embankment, and these innumerable little knolls, thoughts of the crumbled city, levelled themselves to the point of becoming the bare floor of the room.*


♦     I remember, knowing only that it belongs to a memory, this phrase: *"I don't know, but I have the feeling that I'm going to have known."*


♦     Apparently, it has its power in the way verbal inflection declines the present under all the forms of its declension: *"I don't know"* has, by itself, a very sweet attraction; it is the most simple speech; negation collects itself in it to silence itself in making knowledge be silent, and as it can be a response to a determined question ("do you know if . . . ?—I don't know"), it does not pretend to already read the still ambiguous silence, philosophical, mystical, of un-knowledge. *I don't know* is calm and silent. It is a response that no longer is really a part of dialogue: an interruption from which the abrupt character of cessation is withdrawn—as if knowledge and negation made one another more gentle to go as far as a limit where their common disappearance would only be that which escapes. "Not—I know" shows the double power of attack that these two terms maintain when isolated from one another: the decision of knowing, the sharpness of the negative, the edge at which we stop[10] that from all sides impatiently puts an end to everything. "I know" is the sovereign mark of knowing that, in its impersonality and its intemporality, relies on a chance "I" and an already dissipated present: it is the authority, the affirmation not only of knowledge as such, but of a knowledge that wants to know itself. As for negation, its force is that of the forbidden, the summoning of the Law which has always already taken back the lack in the form of the prohibited. "I know—it is forbidden to." *I don't know.* In this response that responds beyond the response, there is no refusal, unless the affidavit, the verification of a relative state of empirical fact, "I don't know, I could, others could, know"), is enough for the modesty of speech. *I don't know* does not verify anything, effaces itself, borne by an echo that does not repeat because what it would repeat holds it back from holding back. Only these two remarks are left for us: how knowledge is sweet when *I don't know;* how negation separates itself from the forbidden when *I don't know* lets it lose itself in the murmuring distance of the separation.

*"I don't know, but have the feeling." But,* even in the form of an addition, is not able to break the silence, only prolongs it further. "I don't know" not being able to repeat itself or to close itself, without running the risk of hardening itself, is indeed the end that does not end. The present that "I don't know" has put gently in parentheses, gives place to a delay, the timid mode of a future that scarcely promises itself, this "feeling" not being an imperfect knowledge or knowledge from sensibility, but the way in which the absence of present dissimulates itself in knowledge itself in letting another still or already absent present come marginally. *"I have the feeling that I am going to have known."* The present, without renouncing granting itself to the present, and as if it held itself back in it still, always leans more towards what in it, already past, indicates itself in the future and gives itself in the immanent approach of a new present (as it must in living temporality), but of a present which, before being there, has already fallen, since "having known", with a swiftness that takes one's breath away, makes time rock in the depths of the past (a past without present). "Having known", the absolute completed of knowledge. "Having known" is in general the proof that there was a moment in which I was he who knew in the present. But, here, *"having known"* has never coincided with a presence, a self present holder of knowledge: beginning from the immanence of a future that I do not touch ("I feel that I am going") and without passing through any actuality, all has collapsed in the irrevocable of the *having known,* and "having known" is not a false appearance, a mockery, the wrinkle of ignorance: having known is a redoubled knowledge, the form

of certitude. There will have been and there has been as an absolute knowledge, which, without being, has always already disappeared through the lack of a subject, either individual or universal, capable of bearing this knowledge in the present.

◆     That the fact of the concentration camps, the extermination of the Jews and the death camps where death continued its work, are for history an absolute which interrupted history, this one *must* say, without, however, being able to say anything else. Discourse cannot be developed from this point. Those who would need proofs will not get any, even in the assent and the friendship of those who have the same thought, there is almost no affirmation possible, because any affirmation is already shattered and friendship sustains itself with difficulty in it. All has collapsed, all collapses, no present resists it.

◆     The awareness at each moment of what is intolerable in the world (tortures, oppression, unhappiness, hunger, the camps) is not tolerable: it bends, sinks, and he who exposes himself to it sinks with it. The awareness is not awareness in general. All knowledge of what everywhere is intolerable will at once lead knowledge astray. We live thus between straying and a half-sleep. To know this is already enough to stray.

◆     Awareness is dreadful, and yet dread does not depend on awareness. Dread without awareness can indeed depend on another form of awareness, that which isolates it, this absolute solitude that comes from awareness and traces a circle around it, the loss of awareness that it entails and that does not diminish it, that is, on the contrary, always more dreadful, the immobility to which it reduces us because it can only be suffered and never suffered enough in a passivity that cannot even promise us the inertia of a dead thing, the muteness that

114

makes it silent even in words, all that makes it escape and that makes everything escape through it; there is, starting from there, a line of demarcation—on one side nobody, on the other, all the others, those who understand, care, live, and understand that also, that there is a line of demarcation, without themselves ever being marked. Dread that conceals and conceals itself. And yet, dread is in relation to all dread, it is the dread of all.

♦ At night, the dreams of death in which one does not know who dies: all, all those who are threatened by death—and oneself, *above the going rate.*

♦ Like a pact with straying, to admit a little lie, a little imposture without the counterpart of what would be the truth; and this allows us to stray only a little without the guarantee of a state in which there is no straying.

♦ That surpasses human force, and yet some man does it, condemned by this not to surpass it.

♦ Why, after death, must all become public, why must the right to publish the least text of Nietzsche or of any writer who would never in his life have accepted its appearing, find an assent in each of us, and even despite us, as if the indestructible affirmed itself in this way? Let us not destroy anything: is it respect, desire to know everything and to have everything, desire to conserve everything in the great archives of humanity, or indeed only the fear, illuminated by a great name, of losing everything, when mortal loss is pronounced? What do we seek in these fragile texts? Something that will not be found in any text, what is outside of text, the word too many, in order that it not fail the completeness of

Complete Works or, on the contrary, so that it always fails it? Or do we give in to the savage force, that which pushes everything outside, that leaves nothing at rest, that prevents anything from at last being silent for an instant?

◆ Behind discourse the refusal to discourse speaks, as behind philosophy the refusal to philosophize would speak: speech not speaking, violent, concealing itself, saying nothing and suddenly crying out. Each is responsible as soon as he speaks, responsibility so heavy that he refuses it, but always in vain, it weighs on him before any refusal, and even if he sinks under its weight, he drags it down with him— responsible, in addition, for his collapse.

◆ What is betrayed by writing is not what writing would have to transcribe and that could not be *transc*ribed, it is writing itself which, betrayed, appeals to laughter, to tears, to passive impassiveness, seeking to write more passively than any passivity.

◆ "I refuse this speech by which you speak to me, this discourse that you offer me to attract me to it in calming me, the time in which your successive words last, in which you hold me back in the presence of an affirmation, is above all this relation that you create between us just by the fact that you address speech to me even in my silence that does not respond."—"Who are you?"—"The refusal to take part in discourse, to make a pact with a law of discourse."—"Do you prefer tears, laughter, immobile madness?"—"I speak, but I do not speak in your discourse: I do not let you, speaking, speak, I force you to speak not speaking; there is no help for you, no instant in which you rest from me, I who am there in all your words before all your words."—"I have invented the great logos of logic that protects me from your incursions and

116

allows me to speak and to know in speaking through the peace of well developed words."—"But I am there in your logic also, denouncing the oppression of a coherence that makes itself the law and I am there with my violence that affirms itself under the mask of your legal violence, that which submits thought to the grip of comprehension."—"I have invented poetic irregularity, the error of words that break, the interruption of signs, the forbidden images, to speak you, and, speaking you, to silence you."—"I am silent, and in the hollowing out of day and night, you hear me, you do nothing but hear me, no longer hearing anything, then hearing everywhere the rumor that has now passed into the world in which I speak with every simple word, the cries of torture, the sighs of happy people, the turbulence of time, the straying of space."—"I know that I betray you."—"You don't have the power to betray me, nor to be faithful to me. I do not know faith, I am not the unspeakable demanding secrecy, the incommunicable that muteness would make manifest; I am not even the violence without words against which you could defend yourself with violence that speaks."—"Nonetheless, affirming when I deny, denying when I affirm, ravaging through an ever thoughtless uprooting: I denounce you as the word never pronounced or still superfluous that would like to except me from the *order* of language to tempt me with another speech. You torment me, it's true, even in leaving me in peace, but I can torment you, too: justice, truth, truth, justice, these terms you reject with your predicatable sneering follow you even to the *other* to which you return them. You do me Good, with your crying of injustice, and I would even say you are the Good that does not let itself be taken for anything good."—"You can say this, I accept everything, acknowledge myself in everything."—"You accept so that I can begin to doubt again the friendship that makes an exception of everything, since your previous refusal, avowal of nothing, was closer to this unique speech that appeals to the Other."—"As you like, I am the Unique."—"No, you will not tempt me with repose in unity; I invoke you beyond this unity, without your knowing it, I beseech you before any beseeching with my obstinate and desolate entreaty."— "This is good, I answer, even before you ask me, and I charge you eternally with the responsibility of my levity."—"I will not obey you, obeying you even in my desire to leave you far from me, turned away from me, in order not to compromise you with my wishes, my strength or the fatigue of my desire: I will always remain indebted to you by the very fact that I acquit myself."—"I accept that also. But, as now I am good and even the good speech, I warn you gently with this precaution: you have simply taken my former place, discourse without discourse, agitated murmur of nights without speech, plaintive rumor both benevolent and malevolent, which stays awake and watches again and again, always listening, in order to make any understanding and any response impossible."—"Yes, I am this murmur, as are you, yet we are always separated from one another, on each side of that which, murmuring, says nothing, oh degrading rumor."—"Marvellous."—"Saying nothing but: *that takes its course.*"

♦　*"You have only to take in the unhappiness of a single person, to whom you are closest, to take in all the unhappiness in one."—"That does not appease me; and how would I dare say that I take in a sole unhappiness where every unhappiness would be taken in, when I cannot even take in my own?"—"Take the unhappy one in in your unhappiness."*

♦　The fragility of what already breaks would respond in the neuter: passion more passive than all that would be passive, yes that says yes before affirmation, as if the passage of dying had always already passed there, before any consent. In the neuter—the name without name—nothing responds, except the response that fails, that has always just missed responding and missed the response, never patient enough to "go beyond", without this "step/beyond" being accomplished. The mirage of passivity is the spontaneity that is almost its opposite: automatic writing, in spite of its difficulties and as risky as it may be, only suspending the rules of appearances (and not attacking—even vainly—the law inscribed at the

118

deepest level) thinks it leaves the movement of writing to its letting go—but writing cannot let itself go, if there is not, for writing, any going—any becoming—to which writing would leave itself, would abandon itself, as if giving its obedience and as happens when one yields to someone's power. And there is no dictation. The dictation of saying has always faded in a previous repetition, since saying can only say again. The resaid of saying tells us something about a passivity— passively ambiguous—where every decision of saying has already fallen. Transgression is not a simple letting go: not that it decides, and, there where it had no hold on anything, by chance and sovereignly, would go beyond the power to do anything even to the impossible. Transgression transgresses by passion, patience and passivity, transgressing always the most passive of ourselves in the "dying by the lightness of dying" that escapes our presence and by which we would escape ourselves without being able to hide ourselves. Passivity, patience, passion, that have renounced the uneasiness of the negative, its impatient shuffling, its infinite wandering, and thus—thus!—would take away from the neuter this retreat in which its negative signaling still leaves it.


◆    *If it were enough for him to be fragile, patient, passive, if the fear (the fear provoked by nothing), the ancient fear that reigns over the city pushing the figures in front of it, that passes in him like the past of his fear, the fear he does not feel, were enough to make him even more fragile, well beyond the consciousness of fragility in which he always holds himself back, but, even though the sentence, in interrupting itself, gives him only the interruption of a sentence that does not end, even so, fragile patience, in the horizon of the fear that beseiges it, testifies only to a resort to fragility, even there where it makes thought mad in making it fragile, thoughtless.*


◆    Fragility that is not that of life, fragility not of that which breaks itself apart, but of the breaking apart, that *I* cannot reach, even in the collapse of the self that gives up and gives its place up to the other.

♦ *Measuring the dimensions of the room that appeared immense to him, he had covered it in several steps: a friend, leaning on the table, his face darkened by sleep, seemed to observe him silently. He resumed his movement, this time incapable of finishing it, of beginning the route, perhaps because of his fatigue, and the fatigue came from his having to delimit the space without taking into account his presence inside it—from a point outside from which the face of his friend, face with eyes closed, suddenly brightened with a smile of kindness.*

♦ Dread, the subterranean world where waking, sleep, cease to be alternatives, where sleep does not put dread to sleep, where, waking, one awakes from dread to dread: as if dread had its day, had its night, its galaxies, its ends of the world, its immobile disaster that lets everything remain.

♦ When one falls—always from high up, no matter how low one is—and a friendly hand suddenly grabs you at the lowest point of the fall, one finally realizes that one is not falling, but was only shrivelled up, immobilized by the feeling of being there wrongly and moving all the less as one should not be there.

♦ *"I am evil, the world attracts me in its evil, and I obscure it with my own, and all the more so because evil preserves in me a self to suffer it."—"You could say the opposite as well, since you are still able to say it."—"I am even more unhappy about this."—"Aren't you forgetting something?"*

♦ Unhappiness is absolute, which does not prevent its being increased—and this sometimes by the very thing that seems to lessen it.

120

♦    Writing slowly to resist the pressure of what is not written, so slowly that, by a frightening reversal, before one even begins, it is beautiful and well written: like he who necessarily becomes anonymous through publication.

♦    Sleep puts dread to sleep and, still, in this state of sleeping dread, one is completely in dread, under its watch that simulates lucidity or makes this active for more dread.

♦    It is not that the anonymous puts a name in a good light, even a name outside of language, as the unprouncable name of God would be, but it is a sign for the absence of name, for the coherence of which this sign remains the sign and which forces the text, published or not, to signal to itself intensely through all that disorganizes it.

♦    Nietzsche dies mad, but dying, for Nietzsche, does not know madness, nor non-madness. In as much as Nietzsche dies in all time outside of time, even if madness overwhelms him, starting from this line of demarcation that the thought of the Eternal Return forces him to cross in an instant, in freeing him from this instant as present, lifting him out of himself as out of madness, by the lightness of dying that the thought of the return trans-lates[11] in leading it falsely—with as much falsity as is necessary to abandon oneself to such a movement—beyond the lightness and to the point at which this lightness regains itself in thought, with all the weight, the slowness, the painful sovereignty of a thought that tries in vain to compensate for its eternal belatedness in regard to dying: to die "mad" would be to die of this lateness, lagging behind dying, which living people who die unaware of their madness take as a sort of anticipated death, which they sanction, visibly or invisibly, by its exclusion.

Nietzsche's madness: as if dying had dangerously eternalized him, either with an eternity of dying, with the ambiguity of eternity, with the danger of the transgression finally accomplished—and then suddenly, having crossed the threshold, handed over to the outside, had led him back by the outside onto the threshold, in the exposedness to which the silence of his stupor reduces him. Madness then means: nobody goes beyond the threshold, except by madness, and madness is the outside that is only the threshold.

◆    *He had never regarded them as anything other than figures that the ancient fear pushed towards him; whence the attraction of beauty and youth that kept him from associating with them, even if their approach, that of the threshold that is neither close nor far, made tempting, yes, like a temptation, the idea of a proximity promised or refused by space, according to the game that is proper to it.*

◆    If the self gives way under the unhappiness of all, it risks being only the self giving way and extended by this unhappiness to the point of becoming the self of everyone, even if it is unhappy. But unhappiness does not authorize the self, the unhappy I, which leads one to think—only to think— that unhappiness has always undone the self, substituting for it the other relation, relation with the other, and that it meanwhile cuts if off in a punctual singularity in which it does not have the right to be a self, even a singular self, not even a suffering self: only capable of feeling to the point of being separated from whatever suffering there is in passivity, whatever common feeling of suffering, and summoned to sustain the relation with the other who suffers by this unsuffered passivity, unauthorized to suffer and as if exiled from suffering.

The *"pas"* of the completely passive—the "step/not beyond"?—is rather the folding back up, unfolding itself, of a relation of strangeness that is neither suffered nor assumed. Transgressive passivity, dying in which nothing is suffered, nothing acted, which is unconcerned and takes on a name only by neglecting the dying of others.

♦    Not "I die", that does not concern me, but "dying that does not concern me" puts me in play in all dying, by way of a relation that does not arrive through me, in bringing me to answer—without responsibility—in the most passive passion, for this relation (relation with the non-concerning) that I neither suffer nor assume. Passivity of dying that does not make me susceptible of dying, nor let me die in others. Dying deliberately for the other, like giving oneself death, at different ethical levels and by acts over which nobody has the power to pass judgement, indicates this moment in which passivity wants to act in its very passivity: that to which practical generosity leads, perhaps, in making real the unrealizable.

♦    To answer for that which escapes responsibility.

♦    Dying: like looking for a displaced subject, a "self-that-dies", as if dying were tired of the lightness proper to it, mark of the unaccomplished trangression (accomplished by its unaccomplishment). Since we would die as if in order to liberate dying, distractedly, heavily, sometimes with the gravity of a responsibility—death heroic, generous, active—, or would die heavy with the anticipated weight of dead things, in giving ourselves up to the inertia of the great repose, dying of inert death and not of passivity—the most passive passion—of dying.

♦    The fragility of dying—that of breaking—does not leave us the right to be fragile, vulnerable, broken, but neither to be strong, indemnable, capable of helping, even to the point of losing the sacrifice.

♦    *"I die, I can do nothing for you but be a burden to you, a painful responsibility, a word that no longer responds to you, the inert thing that you could not love, but only forget even in your memory."—"Dying, you do not die, you grant me this dying as the harmony that surpasses all pain, all solicitude, and in which I tremble softly even in that which rends, at a loss for words with you, dying with you without you, letting me die in your place, in receiving the gift beyond you and me."— "In the illusion that makes you live while I die."—"In the illusion that makes you die while you die."*

◆     Writing: an arrow aiming at the void—the anachronistic of the future-past—and falling always too early, in the too-full of a weighty past, of a future with nothing to come or even worse, in the plenitude of a present that transforms everything into the written rich in resources and in life.

◆     In harmony with the unhappiness of all, this unhappiness that excludes any harmony.

◆     As if awareness were left to us only for us to know what we cannot bear to know.

◆     "Why have written that?"—"I couldn't help it."—"Why does this necessity of writing give place to nothing that does not appear superfluous, vain, and always unnecessary?"— "The necessity was already unnecessary: in the coercion of 'I couldn't help it', there is a feeling even more coercive that this coercion does not have its justification in itself."

◆     *I do not know, but I know that I am going to have known.*

◆     To die freely: illusion (impossible to denounce). For even if one renounces the illusion of believing oneself free in regard

124

to death, one ends up confusing, through constantly belated words, what one calls gratuity, frivolity—its light flame of wanton fire—, the inexorable lightness of dying, with the insubmissiveness of what any act of grasping misses. From which comes the thought: dying freely, not according to our freedom, but, through passivity, abandon (an extremely passive attention), by way of the freedom of dying. And still dying is not only within every power, the impossible in relation to us, that which we cannot take on freely nor suffer under coercion: dying, in the absence of present, in the lack of traces that it leaves, is too light to die, to constitute a dying. This unconsituted-unconsitutuing that touches on the most passive fragility, that undoes and destitutes lavishly, leaving us without recourse, discovering us and giving us over to the discovery of a passion not suffered and of a discourse without words: as soon as we separate ourselves from it, trying to separate it—the unreality of the illusion—it is then that everything turns around: there where there was lightness, there is heaviness; gratuity: responsibility; innocence: sharp putting into question.

◆    Unhappiness: this word that befalls us without giving any explanation and without letting us respond to it, fate without fate. We can do nothing against unhappiness; thus it speaks to us through its muteness. But, even if there is no action capable of effacing it, no gaze to fix it, are we not allowed to feel that there would be a passivity more passive than that by which we suffer it and from which it would be *given* to us to withdraw from it this trait of natural fatality— of a word never pronounced but spoken forever—that it represents to us? *Perhaps* thought is, in its most passive passion, more unhappy than any unhappiness, being unhappy to still be thought in face of the unhappiness that reaches it in others, passivity that leaves a certain distance to respond to it, there where, pretending to escape any cause (social, historical, or ethical) or at least always to surpass it, it affirms itself in its dark sovereignty, in ruins. Yes, perhaps; only perhaps.

♦    To him for whom the longing for unity is the ultimate demand, life, which is living unity, even if only by default, promises happiness and lets itself be lived as supremely happy in its most uncertain moments. The unhappy consciousness, in its division, can indeed tolerate life that lacks unity: it is because of life that it is lived as unhappy and that it projects its ideal of unity, ideal that represents the happy possibility to it—gift, again, of its distress. Unhappiness does not have consciousness to live the happy possibility, nor does it live in the "simple" division—division, it is true, the most pathetically rending because it rends itself—that eternally suffers the reconciliation experienced as eternally deluded longing. Unhappiness passes through the happy consciousness, as through the unhappy consciousness, door open only onto unhappiness.

Freud, thinking of himself, would have said that he who does not feel the need for unity (this need that seemed to him to be tied to philosophy or religion), can accept from the most favorable life only the favor of its melancholy course, with a feeling rather of repulsion and fear before the great moments of exaltation with which it wants to enchant us, as if this exalting gift were a constraint that did not correspond to an appeal, something undesired, a confused submersion of desire. But perhaps it is necessary to say more: we long for unity necessarily through the highest reason, through the strongest desire, thus we must not miss it, nor already suffer from its lack, as we rejoice in that which promises it; only neither unity nor the unique is the ultimate demand, or would be so only for he who could stop at the ultimate of demand, as well as content himself with going back to a first beginning, to what would be original in the origin. The other, in his attraction without attraction, proposes nothing ultimate, nothing that can finish or begin, even if one must have passed through the necessity of the One to know how to respond—response that does not know—to the equivocal appeal of the Other— equivocal, if in the other we cannot be sure that we do not recognize only the still dialectical forms of alterity and never the unknown of the other, outside of the one and of unity. From this perhaps comes the fact that the morcellating demand of writing, across and in the margins of the unity promised by discourse, resonates only distantly with the happiness or unhappiness of life, even in offering life the temptation of another unhappiness, unhappiness without unhappiness, in such a way that not even the consolation of a "profound" unhappiness would be left.

Finally, writing to respond to the unhappy demand, not in harmony with the unhappiness of all, but in the discord of an unhappy little unhappiness.


◆     Unhappiness: perhaps we would suffer it if it struck us alone, but always it reaches the other in us and, reaching us in others, separates us even to this most passive passion in which our lost identity no longer allows us to suffer it, but only to identify ourselves with it, which is outside the identical, to carry us, without identity and without the possibility of acting, towards the other who is always the unhappy one, as the unhappy one is always the other: movement that does not end but, like the "step/not beyond" of the completely passive to which we would respond in dying, gives itself for its own trangression: as if dying, outside of us, consecrated us to the other even in losing us along the way and in holding on to us in this loss.

Unhappiness does not support *itself:* it is in as much as it does not support itself, in the neutral inequality in which it lacks any support as it misses the essence that would show it and would make it be, that it demands to be *borne,* beyond what we suffer, by a trangressive passivity that is never our doing, and whatever we do or do not do, leaves us unprovided for, absent, in the seriousness of a lightness felt as frivolity, in the guilt of an innocence that accuses itself—sharpens itself, puts into question—because it has never "lived" innocent enough. (How could it be lived, if it were not here a matter of the innocence of living, but of the innocence of dying?)


◆     Does the feeling of an absolute lack of communication, of not being able to share unhappiness with the unhappy one, transport "me" into this unhappiness, or does it limit itself to the unhappiness of the incommunicable? Still, "I" am sad in others more than in myself, sad not to be able to lighten this sadness and perhaps to call lack of communication what is still only the inertia of a self that undoes itself and maintains itself in its failure.

♦     The supreme faith of believers: faith at the moment when they will no longer have anything to believe and when they will cease to be believers—faith in death, perhaps, which is hidden from them by faith.

♦     *"Between you and me it is like between something that is more than you and something that is less than me: him and him.—Then you don't really relate yourself to me; the essential has been lost, the unique character of our relationship.—In you, I've freed myself from myself, I no longer make you a slave to the simple consciousness I have of you, nor limit you to yourself in the consciousness you have of yourself.—But I want to be limited and welcomed in the modest unity with which I'm content.—Only one among others, interchangable with others, face among the faces and not even according to the infinitude of your desire.—Yes, that's it, inexchangable in as much as interchangable, the unique someone who recognizes himself only in the unique someone who you are.—Isn't it thus that we meet one another without limiting one another?—How equivocal your answer is!"*

♦     Does not the suffering body force us to live by way of a body that would no longer be neuter, disunified, but in the nostalgia for and the thought of its unity, the "body proper" all the more as it is disappropriated, and giving itself value as it is worth nothing: forcing us to be attentive to ourselves in that which does not deserve any attention? *"From that also, I suf-*

128

*fer, and perhaps, through this suffering mode of life, I break adrift, the rupture is without limit.—You make the most of everything."*

♦     *Oh void in me, into which, in a time more ancient than all ancient times, I threw this self and which, during this time without duration, falls into itself.*

♦     *Think about others in such a way that it is no longer you who comes back from this thought and that it is not in a thought that you dispose yourself towards them.*

♦     *"One's thinking about me makes me feel this self; one's not thinking about me leaves me in this self that exceeds me."—"At least disappear in this thought."*

♦     To live without the hope that life carries, nor with this turning of hope against life (which one calls aggressiveness), is this to live? is it to die? If it is true that it would be absurd to speak of death in terms of life, we do not know if speech itself, and, in speech, something that takes speech away from us and makes us be quiet, is not more related to death and does not lead us, speaking of life, to distance us from hopes, from fears, and from living words, even to this limit that none of us passes alive—except in speech.

♦     Strange threats: *"I don't threaten you, I leave you in the neutrality of a life without threats, which doesn't even leave you a reason to live to defend yourself from the threatening dread.—Then why this dread that surpasses any threat?— Because I threaten you in others, in all that is other, infinite*

129

*field from which the dread that immobilizes you keeps you apart, reducing you to yourself alone, in the solitude of a dread that encloses you because of others.—Dread of all in I who disappear there.—Immured in you by your anguished care for others.—It is because this care has not made use of me enough, has not set to work this patience that would have made me pass beyond.—Don't think you can use others to free yourself from yourself: you are condemned to yourself in order for there still to be someone to welcome others.—But I am nothing, nothing in as much as me.—Nothing, this is what was needed: support the insupportable nothing."*

♦    Dread puts to sleep with a sleep in which it stays awake to keep us entirely in dread: put to sleep for dread.

♦    The tired desire: not only the wearing out of desire in fatigue, not only this turning against itself by which it wears out and wears itself out, but the disappearing of desire in its attempt to maintain itself through the infinity of fatigue, transmitting itself, as fatigue, to the infinity of its wearing out.

Fatigue, fissure, as if, contrary to the movement of etymology, it were fissure, this lack that fails nothing, that would find in fatigue its element of eternity, the illusion of an infinity in the absence of infinity.

♦    There is a moment when generality is frightening: the generality which, whether one likes it or not, one puts to work—using its slightest words, always beyond singularity—and by which one risks generalizing one's own error: fatigue discouraged, as if, without this contribution, the unhappy level of the world could, by a mere nothing, find itself lowered. *"This is because you still attach too much importance to yourself, to your unhappy little share, to your mortal insufficiency,*

130

*to your capacity to be, or not to be, for something, in the common happiness, the common unhappiness.—But, by the mere fact that I exist, at the limit of existence, surviving in survival, I introduce into the circle in which a displaced subject displaces itself something plaintive and impaired—servile perhaps—that is superfluous.—You're not yet at the limit, nor impaired enough, still holding yourself up on your having and your being, nor vulnerable enough, not reaching the point of passivity in which alone the other would reach you without your affecting the other, nor plaintive enough for your cry to carry the plea of all to all.—I know, I still exist too much, of a too little that is too much.—You don't exist, you're dying.—If I were dying, perhaps dying would weigh less, even to the point of interrupting itself, interruption of the dying of others.—Be the lightness of dying, be nothing else for the other, at the risk of 'living' in heaviness, seriousness, responsibility, sharp questioning, that is, in an unhappy incapability of life for yourself."*

♦      *He had lost, before having attained it, this share of impassiveness that would have allowed him not to be unhappy with himself, in order not to increase the general unhappiness: fallen all at once, by an unexpected fall, fortunate and fragile, below impassiveness, without ever being sure that one is at one's most passive and perhaps because there could not be any passivity present there—in the present, in whatever present there is.*

♦      Impassiveness, passivity enclosed in the closure of a self that does not even suffer itself as a self, but wants to free itself from the other in itself, that refuses suffering, far from being exiled from it.

♦      Silence is not the refusal of words: silent from all words, from their reach, from their hearing, from that which, in the least word, has not yet developed itself in speaking ways.

♦ "Death delivers from death.—Perhaps only from dying.—Dying is this lightness within any liberty from which nothing can liberate.—It is this, no doubt, that is frightening in death, contrary to the analyses of antiquity: death does not have within it that with which to allay death; it is thus as if it survived itself, in the powerlessness of being that it disperses, without this powerlessness assuming the task of incompletion—unaccomplishment—proper or improper to dying.—The exteriority of being, whether it takes the name of death, of dying, of the relation to the other, or perhaps of speech when it has not folded itself up in speaking ways, does not allow any relation (either of identity or of alterity) with itself.—With exteriority, speech perhaps gives itself absolutely and as absolutely multiple, but in such a way that it cannot develop itself in words: always already lost, without use and even such that that which loses itself in it (the essence of loss that it would measure) does not claim, by a reversal, that something—a gift, an absolute gift: the gift of speech—is magnified or designated in the loss itself.—*Then I have no right to say anything.—None whatsoever.*"

♦ If speech gives itself to the other, if it is this gift itself, this gift in pure loss cannot *give* the hope that it will ever be accepted by the other, received as a gift. Speech always exterior to the other in the exteriority of being (or of not being) of which the other is the mark: the non-place. *"However, you say that with the assurance of abstract, servile, sovereign words.— In pure loss, in pure loss.—That is still said with too much certainty.—And that also."*

♦ *Every day, doing what he did for the last time, and the night reiterating it without end.*

132

◆ "We should respect in all books, in every speech, something that still demands consideration, a sort of prayer to speech.—I respect it in the least speech, only in the least."

◆ To order is not to speak: nor is to regulate. Language is not an order. Speaking is an attempt (a temptation) to leave this order, the order of language: even if it is by enclosing itself in it. Speaking, this supplication to speak which speech has always rejected, without consideration, or simply led astray, not accepted, not retained.

◆ Friendship: friendship for the unknown without friends.

◆ As if death, through him, distracted itself.

◆ *In this city: by chance; the two young names; immobile facing an immobile friend; the room shrunken, immense: the heavy marble table: the impeded speech: the ancient fear. The Thing remembers us.*

◆ *Coming, coming, signs for the deserted city, signs of themselves: names naming their name. Night after night. We asked ourselves if, in the margin of the book, on the table, we had read it.*

◆ If he writes alone, alone to write, it is because it is better to be alone to lessen the imposture. The imposture: that which imposes itself in the detoured wish of dying (of writing).

♦ *The rumor being only the way in which the city lets it be known that it is deserted, always more deserted.*

♦ *The ancient fear, the aging of the ancient fear. "Are you afraid?"—"With a fear from another time." We were thus, under the guarantee of the young names, the innumerable occupants of fear in this deserted city: hiding fear, hiding ourselves from fear.*

♦ *You would have said in vain: I do not believe in fear; this too ancient fear, without idolatry, without figure and without faith, the beyond of fear that does not affirm itself in any beyond, would again push you into the narrow streets, eternal,* without end, towards *the daily meeting, that which does not propose itself to you as an end; whence the fact that, even making your way there every day, you are never there. "Because I reach it by flight, fleeing it endlessly."*

*"You respect fear.—Perhaps, but it does not respect me, it has no regard."* The most serious of idolatries: to have regard for that which has no regard.

♦ *Who would believe that I am close to you?*

♦ If to live is to lose, we understand why it would be almost laughable to lose life.

♦ *He could neither pronounce nor silence the two names, as if these in their day to day banality had always run through language to except themselves from it. Figures, pushed here and there by the dry wind, this wind of rumor letting it be known that the deserted city could not do without the illusion of a tomb.*

134

♦     They inspire you.—Strange inspiration that I would receive only in expiring.—Inspiration is indeed that: the chance, the time of an expiration in which every word would be breathed to you before being given to you.

Writing always more easily, more quickly than he writes.


♦     One must not fix the saying-between in the forbidden[12], but "one must not", where do you situate it, how do you say it if not as the forbidden that has already turned into a negative prescription, fulfilling the prohibition, making it a fulfillment, the separation of the saying-between.


♦     *Taking three steps, stopping, falling, and, all of a sudden, becoming sure of himself in this fragile fall.*


♦     To survive, not to live, or, not living, to maintain oneself, without life, in a state of pure supplement, movement of substitution for life, but rather to arrest dying, arrest that does not arrest, making it, on the contrary, *last*. *"Speak on the edge[13]—line of instability—of speech." As if it attended the exhaustion of dying, as if the night, having started too early, at the earliest time of day, doubted it would ever become night.*


♦     It is almost certain that at certain moments we notice: speaking again—this survival of speech, sur-speech—is a way of letting ourselves know that for a long time we have no longer spoken.


♦     Praise from the near to the far.


♦     Come, come, come [*viens, viens, venez*][14], you whom the injunction, the prayer, the wait could not suit.

135

♦     "Be at peace with yourself.—There is no one in me to whom I can speak familiarly.—Be at peace.—Peace, this war that is only appeased.—Be at peace, without peace without war, outside of any page to write, outside of any pact to sign, outside of texts and of countries.—The outside does not promise any peace.—Be, without knowing it, at peace with yourself, in the beyond of peace that you would not know how to reach.—That which you promise, I don't desire.—Accept without desire the promise I make you."

Outside of any mercenary speech, silence without refusal gives thanks.


♦     *There had been something like an event: the unforeseeable without complaint, keeping itself out of sight. Yes, that is what it was about; what was it about? As if death, completed, had left everything intact, only free of everything, acquitted of this dying for which the speech maintained within silence had amicably persisted. Thus, the false appearances* seemed *to have left him; and that, this freeing from the debt of secret and regret, movement of immobility, far from truth and appearance, apart from play and openness, definite slowness, repose without the promise of leisure, with the inescapable tranquility: gift of serenity on the face henceforth entirely visible, escaping the evasive.*

*Shadow of time, of old, welcome their figures. Respond no longer to the one who would keep memory captive.*


♦     Both in distress, the narrow march of their fragile fall, common: death dying, side by side.


♦     *Coming towards us, as they came towards one another through this plurality that unifies them without showing unity: their young return.*

*He thought, saving the we, like he believed he saved thought in identifying it with the fragile fall, that their young return would allow him, even in their no longer being together (for a long time he had no longer heard anything, not even an echo, that could have passed for an approbation, a confirmation of the daily meeting), to fall in community. Fragile fall— common fall: words always skirting one another.*

*And he knew, thanks to the too ancient knowledge, effaced by the ages, that the young names, naming twice, an infinity of times, one in the past, the other in the future, that which is found only on this side, that which is found only beyond, named hope, deception. Hand in hand, from threshold to threshold, like immortals, one of whom was dying, the other saying:* "would I be with whom I die?"

♦ *"Why do you no longer say anything?"—"Have I ever said anything?"—"You let speak, without anything being said, in the way of a thank you, the hope, the deception of every utterance."*

*"Why do you no longer say anything?"—"Indeed, to be able still to repeat this question in a low voice, lower each time: a voice clear, neuter, impeded."—"I no longer have, even in the form of this last question, any thought that concerns you."—"It is good to renounce keeping us together in the discernment of a thought."—"Why do you give back to me, under the illusion that it is good, what I no longer know how to give?"—"It is good."*

*He was so calm in dying that he seemed, before dying, already dead; after and forever, still alive, in this calm of life for which our hearts beat—thus having effaced the limit at the moment in which it is it that effaces.*

*(In the night that is coming, let those who have been united and who efface one another not feel this effacement as an injury that they would inflict on one another.)*

♦ Free me from the too long speech.

# NOTES TO THE TRANSLATION

1. I have translated "le 'il'" as "the he/it" throughout because "il" is both the masculine personal third person pronoun and the impersonal third person pronoun. Since there is no neuter pronoun in French, Blanchot uses "le 'il'."

2. The phrase thus rendered is "le moi n'est pas moi mais le même." "Même" means both "same" and "self." Blanchot questions the identity of the self as a model for identity as a whole. The self, rather than being a model for identity, means only the sameness of the self-same, and as such becomes what Blanchot calls "a canonic abbreviation for a rule of identity."

3. What I have translated as "familiarity" throughout is "tutoiement" which means the use of the familiar form of address, through the use of the pronouns "tu" and "toi." Generally, the use of the familiar form indicates some kind of intimacy with or closeness to the person so addressed, but in the case of the law, the familiar form is used only to exclude any closeness.

4. I have translated "la chance" as "luck" and "le hasard" as "chance." "La chance" in French has the meaning of both "luck" and "chance" in English, which gets somewhat lost in the translation due to the necessity of using "chance" in English for "le hasard," which means "chance" in the sense of randomness.

5. Blanchot plays here on the verbs "tenir," "to hold" or "to hold on" and "entretenir," "to maintain," "to entertain," "to converse with" and their noun forms "tenue" and "entretien."

6. "Franchissement," from the verb "franchir" means "crossing." "Franchise" means openness or candor.

7. "La perte est exigence, elle exige de la pensée qu'elle soit dé-pensée. . . ." "Dépensé" means "spent," but with the hyphen, it attaches the pronoun "de" to the word "thought."

8. There is a multiple play on words in the phrase *entre: entre ne(u)tre*. In the first place, "entre" is both the second person, familiar form of the imperative of the verb "to enter" (which also occurs in the first person plural in the word with which the book begins, "entrons") and the adverb "between." "N'être" is the negative of the verb "to be" and an anagram of "entre"; with the insertion of the "u" "n'être" becomes "neutre."

9. I have left "jouissance" and "*re*jouissance" untranslated because in translating them the sense of repetition would be lost. "Rejouissance" as Blanchot uses it here indicates a repetition of

"jouissance," or sexual pleasure and expenditure, but in its usual usage it means "rejoicing," a public, rather than private, pleasure.

10. What I have translated as "the edge at which we stop" is Blanchot's word "l'arrête," which does not exist as a word, but is a combination of two words. The first of these is "l'arrêt," which can mean a place to stop, an arrest in the police sense, or a judicial sentence, as in Blanchot's title *L'Arrêt de mort*. The word "arête," on the other hand, indicates a sharp edge (it can also means a fish bone on which one risks choking). Blanchot takes the same word later in the text, where he qualifies it as "line of instability".

11. "Tra-duire," "to translate," means literally "to lead across."

12. "Il ne faut pas figer l'entre-dire en interdit." "Entre-dire" and "interdire" are semantically the same, since "inter" means "between."

13. See note 10.

14. "Viens" and "venez" are, respectively, the singular and plural forms of the imperative of the verb "to come." It sounds as if two people are addressed, each separately, and then together.